CREATION SOUNDS

Music, Gender and Performativity in Contemporary Latin American Literature

---

Maria L. Figueredo

CREATION SOUNDS

Music, Gender and Performativity in Contemporary Latin American Literature

Maria L. Figueredo

COMMON GROUND RESEARCH NETWORKS 2018

First published in 2018
as part of the New Directions in the Humanities Book Imprint
doi: 10.18848/978-1-61229-951-8/CGP (Full Book)

Common Ground Publishing
2001 S. 1st St., Suite 202
University of Illinois Research Park
Champaign, IL
61821

Library of Congress Cataloging-in-Publication Data

Names: Figueredo, Maria (Maria L.), author.
Title: Creation sounds : music, gender and performativity in contemporary
    Latin American literature / Maria L. Figueredo.
Description: Champaign, IL : Common Ground Research Networks, 2018. |
    Includes bibliographical references and index.
Identifiers: LCCN 2018022387 (print) | LCCN 2018046516 (ebook) | ISBN
    9781612299518 (pdf) | ISBN 9781612299495 | ISBN 9781612299495 (hardback
    : alk. paper) | ISBN 9781612299501 (paperback : alk. paper)
Subjects: LCSH: Latin American literature--History and criticism. | Music and
    literature--Latin America.
Classification: LCC PQ7081 (ebook) | LCC PQ7081 .F46 2018 (print) | DDC
    860.9/3578098--dc23
LC record available at https://lccn.loc.gov/2018022387

Cover Photo Credit: Maria L. Figueredo

Table of Contents

Acknowledgements ix

Author's Note xi

Introduction 1

Chapter 1 9
Matrilineal Songs and Storytelling: Inés Arredondo, "Canción de Cuna"

Chapter 2 25
Poetic Bodies, Soundscapes and the 'World Wide Womb': Nadia Prado, Malú Urriola, Cecilia Vicuña

Chapter 3 49
Performative Reading and the Multimedia Novel: Laura Esquivel's La ley del amor

Chapter 4 65
Sound Memory and Textual Tango: Mario Benedetti and Winston Mombrú

Chapter 5 79
E-Poetry: Videopoetry, Text, Aurality and Music in Rocío Cerón, Lía Colombino and Melisa Machado

References 103

Acknowledgements

I would like to thank all those who have contributed to reading and providing valuable feedback to make this book possible. First I would like to thank my family, friends and students who through the years have shared insights with me and enriched this book through dialogue, reflection and experiences related to its themes. In particular also I especially thank those who assisted in reading the final drafts; their comments and feedback influenced this book in many ways. Finally I would like to achknowledge the role that music has played in my life and the way it has always served to elucidate, lift and encourage me when words were not enough or when they became tangled in cultural inbetweenness.

Author's Note

An associate professor in the Spanish Program of the Department of Languages, Literatures and Linguistics at York University, Canada, I teach courses in Spanish language and culture, and in Spanish American literature. At York University I am also a Research Fellow at the Centre for Research on Latin America and the Caribbean (CERLAC), and on its executive board. I have been a Senior Fellow at Massey College, University of Toronto, since 2009.

Specialized in the relationship between literature and music, particularly on the convergences of these arts since the twentieth century, my research has examined the ways these arts find points of contact and the effects on cultural perceptions of literature. Beginning with case studies and field research that examined the poetic and musical links of the intersections between oral traditions and writing, I have also studied the historical intricacies of the relationship of literature to music in Latin America and on women's writing and gender issues. More recently, shifts in the technological influences of the internet and other media on the production and reception of literature have expanded this work to include networked poetries, video-poems, gaming theory as applied to poetry, and poetry installations and literary innovation. My work in these areas, including on music as a subtext in women's prose and music in the 20th century Latin American novel, has been collected in edited book volumes, scholarly journals, conference proceedings and online forums. My first book, Poesía y canto popular: Su convergencia en el siglo XX. Uruguay, 1960-1985 (Poetry and Popular Song: Their Convergences in the 20th Century, 2005) was the first systematic study to examine poetry that was set to music in times of political crisis in Uruguay; based on extensive field research, this study revealed the collaborations between poetry and music as alternative response, resistance, and defense of social justice, elaborating further dialogue on the relationship between these arts.

A classically trained guitarist and singer-songwriter, I have recorded and performed in Canada, Brazil and Uruguay and shared resources with musicians in each of these countries. My passion for teaching has also bridged with this arena, and has led me to create and organize a host of cross-cultural events featuring musicians, spoken word, writers, and lectures on these topics and related fields.

A member of the League of Canadian Poets, my poetry has appeared in Jones Av. V/2, in a compact disc compilation titled The Sound of Poetry, and in the first trilingual anthology of Hispano-Canadians writers and artists, ANTARES (2009): Anthology of Hispanic-Canadian Literary and Artistic Creativity. In 2015, I edited Poet-Tree 2015: The Poetry of Sport & The Sport of Poetry as the creator/lead of an Ignite community project for the Toronto 2015 Pan American/Parapan American Games, that contained works by salient poets working in Latin America today; the edition broke new ground as few volumes exist that connect poetry and sports. It also was exciting as the project brought together a group of authors from various generations, backgrounds and artistic expression from over 40 countries. The full text of the book is available here: https://spanish.dlll.laps.yorku.ca/files/2016/03/Poet_Tree_Full_e_book.pdf

For further details, please see: https://profiles.laps.yorku.ca/profiles/mfiguere/.

Introduction

This book considers the role of music and aurality in the multi-mediated reception that privileges the performative elements of meaning production, thereby affecting literary culture. By examining literary trends and the interactions of innovations by writers in Latin America with music, the interplay of the post-postmodern, transnational word is channeled in relation to visual, performative, cybernetic and non-linear artistic expressions of literature produced since the latter half of the 20th century. Intertextual relationships between the historical weight of previous influential voices in the Latin American literature, juxtaposed with twenty-first-century acts of writing and sounding out music's role within the literary text, mix together with meta-histories and physical action, co-existing and inhabiting plural spaces onsite and online. The mediation of digital technologies expand literature in its encounter with sound and image and beyond a specifically bound site; however, the presence, or irruption, of musical allusions and references to sound within the literary text is at the heart of our discussion, as are the performances of those works.

The present work includes bibliographical data garnered from literary criticism published between 2007 and 2016 on the area of the relationship between literature and music, particularly with the emphasis on: (a) the musicalization of the novel in contemporary Latin American writing; (b) the incorporation of poetry, visuals and musical accompaniment to the production of literary texts and the ways this shifts the reader-text relationship and the considerations of the nature of the literary text; (c) discussions on the performativity of reading and the role of musical elements in the phenomenology of the text.

A second significant feature of my project here is to connect the phenomenon to theories of agency from a gendered consciousness. As in the works of Kristeva, Irigaray, Butler, Spivak and Athanasiou, this approach aims to interrogate these new forms of literary art making in terms of its dismantling of binarisms and to rethink bodies from "the in-between position" (Bloodsworth, 2007, 2). This aspect takes issues with the stability of gender conceptions vis-à-vis the discursive event; as artist Lauren Wilson suggests, this process of analysis involves "digressions that are obsessive, introspective, and therefore difficult to unravel. The intention is not to exhibit a linear view, but to open up awkward political questions. This happens though a viewers' attempt to classify the works [in an] overly specific state of flux" (2014). How does this classification close or open up the literary work for bodies in action and in relation to each other? How do its embodied aspects transfer across time and space?

Finally, this book offers a contribution to the study of literary form, by understanding the encounter between experimental and experiential literature organized by emerging writers in collaboration with other artists, in joint installation projects and "urban interventions," collage poems, spoken word, performative readings, multidisplinary exhanges between the visual spatial aspects of the literary word in action. This raises questions such as: How are authors involved in questioning the nature of creative practice and the definition of the "literary" work in the 21st century from Latin American and international perspectives respectively? Modes such as interdisciplinary performance strategies that integrate films, photographs, paintings, poem-collages, installation art, sculpture, spoken word, music, compact disc recording inserts, mp3 data and other electronic media such as "Motionpoems," or a revamping of traditional salon readings, created by the certain writers in the twenty-first century poetry in action, provide contextual grounding for the cultural, historical and social threads that emerge from the literary works. In what ways do the crossings between literature as written act, spoken act, silent act, and visual act, performativity and non-performativity, the 'sayable' and the 'unsayable' for example, allow 'readers/audiences/participants' to explore the imaginary space between art and life, the politics of poetry as event, and the idea of 'non art' versus 'art' from the literary perspective?

The book takes a site-specific and body-centred approach. Forerunners of literature in multimedia formats have been studied in relation to individual authors and identity politics (Coonrod Martínez 2010; *Rodríguez* 2010, such as Mexican author Laura Esquivel's *La ley del amor (1995)* [*The Law of Love*, 1996]. The ways that this writer integrates music, comic strips and other devices (such as an accompanying CD-ROM with tracks of popular Caribbean *danzones* recorded by Argentine Liliana Felipe, a piece by Cuban pianist Oscar M. Bouffartique, and arias from Puccini's best known operas), with transgendered, "body-swapping" (Taylor 2002, 2014) characters have been explored in my research (Figueredo 2011, 2014). Principally this work has centered on the performativity of reading as an innovative practice; Esquivel was among the first to implement the incorporation of a compact disc to the reading experience. Engaging readers in alternative ways raises questions about the nature of the text that have since become embedded in notions related to hypertext, e-poetries and digital installations. More traditional forms of poetry as performance, installation art and happenings tie now in with increased virtual spaces of engagement, and transnational approaches.

Poetry events held in post-dictatorially marked spaces of Latin America, such as Chile, by Nadia Prado and Malú Urriola in *"Poesía es +"* [Poetry is + (more)] (2002), and in the US by Chilean-born Cecilia Vicuña in *Cloud-Net* (1999) and *The Menstrual Quipu* (2006), question social, economic, and environmental threats. These poets posit a different "wor(l)d-making," by engaging with power centres of public decision-taking: this is yet to be fully examined and contrasted with other works of poetry in action. There is yet to be a critical in-depth study of the phenomenon of the digital innovations by these poets and their reach into other markets and readerships. How do the poets do so in various geo-political settings? What is the relation of the characteristics of these works to other manifestations of performances in other settings such as North American in which poetry and and song and/or music are linked?

For example, in 2014, the Arts of Time Ensemble based in Toronto, Canada included in its programming a concert featuring Canadian author Margaret Atwood titled "The Poem / The Song." In this event held November 7-8, poems by Leonard

Cohen, Margaret Atwood, T.S. Eliot, August Kleinzahler, Johnny Mercer, Petrarch and What Whitman were performed by six musicians (on pinao, violin, bass, saxophone, cello and guitar) and three singers. In the programming guide the information provided about the concept and performative quality of the concert reads as follows: "The interconnectedness of music and poetry is examined in a program that presents poetry in a variety of musical settings and music inspired by the poem" (2014, 3). Cohen's work is described in the final line of the description as "the ultimate marriage of poetry and music" (3).

Communicative strategies such as poetry art actions and multimedia enhanced novels harness the power of performativity in literature and its contacts with the other arts; in this trans-artistic move, which Judith Butler, Julia Kristeva, Luce Irigaray and other poststructuralist and feminist philosophers and theorists maintain have an impact on political imaginaries, not just to amuse, entertain and comment, but to generate new actions. My project proposes to compare and contrast the use of the arts—poetry-based, though not confined to the traditional book in print format—in forming supports to writing and its promotional reach—in its appearance and its agency for possible actions in the world, and from the perspective of shared affect. Furthermore, in approaching memory, the project takes the position that "most of our history in not linear" (Ralston Saul 2002,16) and of "seeing in the round" (Ralston Saul 15). This type of seeing from at least two perspectives at once is a release from "absolute truth" (ibid) or "ideology" (Ralston Saul 16). How does music's role in literature capture these perspectives, and how are cultural legacies pervasive or countered in the modes of production, themes, lyrical voices and plural subjects prevalent in each body of work by these writers?

The theoretical framework operative here bridges the above communicative strategies with current innovation in literature, so as to ascertain the following: How does music "do" something in literature? For this portion of the book's questions, certain theories relating to perception in reading reception and creation (Haupt 2014; Goodchild 2012) and reality-making (Turok, 2012; Hawking and Mlodinow 2012; Hunt, 2009; László 2008), connections to the psychologies and politics of space and embodiment (Bachelard 1994; Butler 2006; Foucault 1990; Kristeva 2000) come into play, as well as hypertext theory (the connection between literary theory and computer technology (Correa-Díaz and Weintraub, 2010, 2016a, 2016b; Landow 2006; Pequeño Glazier 2001; Simanowski 2016; Taylor 2002, 2014; Taylor and Pitman 2008). Chilean (Nadia Prado, Malú Urriola, Cecilia Vicuña), Mexican (Rocío Cerón), Uruguayan (Melisa Machado, Mario Benedetti) and Paraguayan poetry (Lía Colombino) today grounds the discussion in the particularities of individual works. Another aspect that surfaces in the reading dialectics and performance dynamics of each work is in relation to culture as a resource and political agency (Butler and Spivak 2007; Butler and Athanasiou 2013; Yépez 2013; Yúdice 2003) to invoke the complexities of the experience. In addition, the book explores how these responses are shaped individually, even though they are subsumed in a world of collective values and justice, as seen in Laura Esquivel's and Inés Arredondo's works from Mexico, and in Mario Benedetti's works from Uruguay.

Overall, the aims are, based on the following lines of questioning: 1) To examine the effects of these literary and musical interactions in literature; and 2). To trace links found in their works thematically and circumstantially. By examining texts in light of these thematic threads, the book explores the following questions:

a) How do the incursions of sound elements, musical references and reading with multimedia components (e.g. CD-ROM, mp3s, cyber presences) empower through affect and influence the reception of poetry in Spanish America?
b) How can multimedia reading or performed literature alter the perception of memory and agency, and how do they enhance, alter or transfer some or any of the effects of gender identity and social, economic, political or physical situadedness?
c) How do the above, in concert with each other, relate to notions of individual versus plural expression, community, cultural legacy, memory, social and political empowerment?
d) What evidence is there of particularly Spanish American ways of incorporating music in literary texts?

Close readings and hermeneutic analysis allow me to contrast how these authors merge the literary with music and interactivity of reading and writing not only for artistic merit but as agents of change and democratic evolution and particularly with the innovations in new media. Former studies (such as those I have conducted of Arentinian hypertext artist Belén Gache in 2008, 2013; of Esquivel in 1995 and 2013; of Prado and Urriola in 2002; and of Vicuña in 2012 and 2014) involving other genres of literature as well, inform the baseline methodology.

Also, this book examines music's role in literature in light of recent reports (*Digital Latin American Network* 2013) and new critical theory on the digital in literary studies, such as *Poetry and Digital Poetics* (Correa-Díaz and Weintraub, 2016); *Cybertext Poetics: The Critical Landscape of New Media Literary Theory* (Eskelinen, 2012); *Digital humanities and digital media conversations on politics, culture, aesthetics, and literacy (Simanowksi, 2016)*. The emphasis on locating the body in social space is fundamental to understanding this interaction of music and literature, as well as the repercussion of the effects of media culture from a specific cultural perspective, such as that of Spanish American writers. It is here that we will focus on the interstices of sound, textual communication and quantum field physics applied to literary theory that authors in Spanish America have pioneered as fields of experience and experimentation for creating reality or proposing alternative realities in creative sound-textual ways.

In a previous book, *Poesía y canción popular: Su convergencia en el siglo XX* [*Poetry and Popular Song: Their Convergence in the Twentieth Century*] (Montevideo: Linardi y Risso, 2005), I examined the ways poets and musicians in twentieth century Latin America had created methods of resistance and protest through poetry and music and performance in specifically challenging socio-political circumstances, and had employed the case study of Uruguay (1960-85) to track some of these effects and specific interactions between social, political and artistic perspectives of reality and their outcomes. Previous work in this area also included as part of a 43-page annotated bibliography titled: *York Resources for Research in the Relationship of Literature and Music in Spanish America, Complete Bibliography* (2008). In subsequent publications I have continued my work in this area by examining other texts, authors, contexts and genres, which has been published in scholarly journals, edited volumes and conference proceedings. These publications have included the study of music as a subtext in women's prose, music in the 20th century Latin American novel, e-poetry, and the relationship of poetry performance and music.

In this book, I propose to focus on contemporary renditions of the themes by linking them with the overarching method of reality making through music's liberating power to merge the 'sayable' and the 'unsayable' that is at the heart of the truth sought in these textual creations. The chapters provide a holistic view of the relationship of literature and music in Spanish American in the latter half of the twentieth century and early part of the new millennium, and of the way technological and social change co-evolve and impact on literary production and reading reception.

The first chapter's focus on Inés Arredondo's "Canción de Cuna" and its association to matrilineal songs and (his)stories traces the power of the mother tongue in identity and subject creation. Musical References in the Identity-Formation of the Subject in Inés Arredondo's Short Story "Canción de Cuna" ['Lullaby'] reveals the lineage of female subjects established through music, and its antidote to familial storytelling. A close reading of this short story by Mexican author Inés Arredondo examines how language, power and identity interact in a first-person narrative of a third-generation member of a German immigrant family in Mexico. The incorporation of songs in German and Spanish reveal the liberation available to the female subject through musical expression as it serves to release blocked memories and build connections to lost family ties.

In Chapter 2, "Poetic Bodies, Soundscapes and the 'World Wide Womb'," I discuss the pulsations of the *chora* and quantum quarks in relation to the intersection of the materiality and the ephemerality of the body in determining reality. For this purpose, the Chilean poetic art actions of Malú Urriola, Nadia Prado and Cecilia Vicuña serves as case studies that set out the possibility that poetry, while ephemeral, can affect and critically subvert current notions of realism. By questioning contemporary positions of power, performance and gender, their acts of remembering and healing through poetry move into sound and gesture as liberating forcefields. The art acts of Prado and Urriola in their four-part series titled *Poesía es +* [Poetry Is More] and Vicuña's *Cloud-Net* comment upon the post-dictatorial and post-9/11 Chilean landscape in particular, and the world wide reach of neoliberalism in general.

Chapter 3, "Performative Reading and the Multimedia Novel" explores Mexican writer Laura Esquivel's *La ley del amor* (1995) in which the musical word as release connects with notions of presence, myth and ecstatic narrative. It also highlights a performativity of reading that is required to complete Esquivel's novel with compact disc. In *La ley del amor* [*The Law of Love*] her second novel, the bestselling author of *Like Water for Chocolate* takes the reader through a tripartite construction of narrative text, music and comic strips woven into a complex web of signification. Retrieving a mythical/historical archive of Mexican colonial and postcolonial references via a sci-fi romp across seven centuries, from 1527 to 2180, the characters of *La ley del amor* are cross-gendered, hybrid constructions that challenge the reader to re-enact the story line by dancing at specific moments, imagining memories alongside musically-accompanied "regressions" and tuning in to *danzones*, arias and the poems of the nahuas of the *Cantares mexicanos*. Since its publication few novels have appeared in this multimedia format, with accompanying compact disc containing songs and sound effects, comic "clips" and musical meta-textual references. Recent examples, such as Joseph Coulson's *Of Song and Water* (2007), which integrate jazz improvisational techniques in literary language, come closer to Latin American novels by authors such as Julio Cortázar (*El perseguidor*, for instance) where a "musical" reality superimposes itself on other perspectives. Jodi Picoult's *Sing you Home* (2011) comes with a cd as *La ley del amor* did, and accentuates the sonorous elements for its own narrative purposes. While some critical attention has been bestowed upon questioning body-identity associations in the novel, such as in Claire Louise Taylor's "Body-Swapping and Genre-Crossing" (2002), there has been less focus on the sensory interplay of the reading of Esquivel's novel and its implications for literary culture's creative power to displace hegemonic, pre-established colonialist and postcolonial dualisms. This section examines the performativity of reading and its transformative capacity to displace previous notions of reality-making and guide readers to new experiences of inscribing alternative realities in their own bodily response to the text.

Chapter 4, "Sound Memory and Performing Tango in Mario Benedetti's novel *La borra del café*," analyzes the appearance of a tango scene in a chapter of a 1992 novel by well-known Uruguayan author Mario Benedetti. Set in an auto-fictional style, the novel's use of tango in its 29th chapter, titled "El surco del deseo" [The Groove of Desire], deconstructs the linguistic stability of the narrative discourse with its allusions to music and dance. The various levels in which this musical subgenre is relevant for the thematic thrust and the reconstruction of memory via sound and dance imagery find alliances in the discontinuities and breaks of gramatical structures in the text. This renders a need to read between the lines, rhythmically and allegorically.

Chapter 5, "E-Poetry: Videopoetry, Text, Aurality and Music in Rocío Cerón, Lía Colombino and Melisa Machado" explores envisions how the online and on site works of contemporary Latin American poets from Mexico, Paraguay and Uruguay respectively, engage with discrete elements of sound, gesture, visual and historical framing to intersect with the poetic word and produce overflows of meaning across various geo-political spaces. By rethinking the staticity of the body in each reading/viewing experience, poems by these women writers reflect shifting notions of self across time and space, including ambiguous gendered positions of the poetic subject. The interpolation of the body is a function of the performance of the poetry (poetry as an oral act) and a function of the representation of the (real, natural, creaturely) body (as opposed to the ideal body, mechanistic-linguistic projection of the mind) within the poems themselves. By examining how these poets represent their countries in specific international events captured online, we see the attempt to salvage excessive ruptures of the relational self across time and space.

More broadly, my book continues to dialogue about the ways that literature and music intersect, a topic that seems as old as the origins of the genres themselves, and yet that even today raise questions. With the bestowing of the Nobel Prize for Literature recently on popular musician, singer-songwriter and activist Bob Dylan (1941-), the topic continues to evoke intriguing debates on where literature ends and music begins. As Marcelo Pereira has recently noted in an article about the selection of Dylan as the 2016 Nobel laureate, the innovations that this American artist produced in his works have, directly or indirectly, left an indelible impression on contemporary artists and on generations to come:

> desde el hecho mismo de abrir un enorme espacio para la libertad creativa hasta el establecimiento de diversos modelos de texto que él legitimó y que se han convertido en subgéneros. Por esos caminos que Dylan abrió fueron después John Lennon, Chico Buarque, Leonard Cohen y prácticamente todos los grandes autores de letras de canciones. (2016)

> (from the very fact of clearing an enormous space for creative freedom to the establishment of diverse models of texts that he legitimized and that have become subgenres. The paths that Dylan cleared later ushered in John Lennon, Chico Buarque, Leonard Cohen and practically all of the great songwriters of our times.)

Even those who are not musicians and writers have felt the impact of Dylan's lyrics. In what Pereira terms a "cascading effect of positive consequences in the field of song" 2016) even more people have felt the reach of his social, political and personal messages. As Pereira aptly expresses, Dylan's "songs contain narrations of great potency and dozens of phrases that condense profound concepts or are extremely moving - in both rational and emotional ways – because of the refined and innovative use of words. What else are we talking about when we say 'literature'?" (ibid).

In addition to examining the various ways that music can interact with literary works, this book makes available (some for the first time) in English translation to a wider audience, the poetry, prose and multimedia productions of Latin Americans writers who are among the most salient and innovative of the twentieth and twenty-first centuries.

Creation Sounds

CHAPTER 1

Matrilineal Songs and Storytelling

THE POWER OF THE MOTHER TONGUE

Prior to acquiring verbal language and to participating fully in a system of pre-established linguistic signs of communication, we are. We have a notion of being in relationship with others and with a physical, emotional, geographical, mental space of connection and response to stimuli. What we do not yet have, if we are not participants in a community of shared verbal language, is full access to the power to negotiate for our position therein. However, if power is indeed more fully realized by managing the skills of linguistic communication, who among us cannot also agree that sometimes to speak works against that power or places us in a position of disadvantage, vulnerability or danger vis-à-vis those who hear us or believe to have understood what we intended to communicate. If identity is based on an unstable set of coordinates between negotiating self-awareness and communication with the world around us and in communities in which we can gain access through common language, then that identity can be somewhat shaped by the dialogue with others, albeit ambiguously or tenuously at times, and for certain not wholly independent. What becomes the main goal of this dialogue is action, that of ourselves or that of influencing others to act, so that we can realize what is our desire or respond to our interrogatives about the world in which we experience life as we know it. The word "power" in Spanish is translated as "poder," which is a noun and an infinitive verb, generative of the action, "to be able to." Thus the implied transference of wielding power and a direct ability to accomplish our intent, is inherent in this set of meanings.

In *Giving an Account of Oneself* (2005) Judith Butler discusses the process by which the self is determined. Responsibility ultimately lies in each subject, regardless of the contextual coordinates and power relations and meanings existing prior to its arrival in the world. In particular Butler examines "Foucault's view [that...] calls into question the limits of established regimes of truth" (24) and that this questioning "by which my own truth is established is motived by the desire to recognize another or be recognized by one" (24). By extension, Butler affirms this as an,

> effort to escape or overcome the terms by which subjectivation takes place, my struggle with norms is my own. [Foucault's] question effectively remains, 'Who can I be, given the regime of truth that determines ontology for me?' He does not ask the question 'Who are you?' nor does he trace the way in which a critical perspective on norms might be elaborated starting out from either of those questions. (Butler, 2005: 25)

Placed within the wider framework of ethical questions, Butler presents interesting connections for our discussion of Arredondo's literary text in relation to the theme of language in identifying oneself as subject. For Arredondo, stories are less about social and political commentary or denunciation than about examining how these aspects play into the self and its becoming aware of its complex relation to others.

Arredondo states in an interview given to Erna Pfeiffer in 1989 and published in *EntreVistas: Diez escritoras mexicanas desde Bastidores* (Vervuert: Frankfurt am Main, 1992) that her short stories are

> Pura ficción, puro juego estético, pura literatura, no hay intenciones sociales ni nada. Cuando fui a dar unos cursos en Philadelphia, un maestro mexicano que estaba allí me dijo que cuando había pasado por mi tierra, había visto que las mujeres iban al río a lavar y que transportaban agua en cubetas para su casa, que por qué yo no denunciaba eso y le dije: yo no estoy para denunciar, que denuncien los periodistas, yo estoy para hacer literatura. Si eso me sirve, lo agarro, pero mientras no me sirva, no tengo por qué explicar por qué no hay servicios hidráulicos en la colonia que tú viste, ¿no? No quedó muy conforme, pero, en fin…" (18).

> (Pure fiction, pure aesthetic play, pure literature, there are no social intentions or anything. When I went to teach some courses in Philadelphia, a Mexican educator who was present told me that when he'd passed through my land, he had seen that women went to the river to wash and they transported water on buckets on their heads to their homes, that why did I not denounce this and I told him: I am not here to denounce, let the journalists denounce, I am here to do literature. I that serves me in some way, I take it, but if it does not, I do not have to explain why there are no hydraulic services in the neighbourhood you saw, no? He was not too satisfied with my answer, oh well…) [translation mine]

And yet each of Arredondo's stories reflect upon the intimate expereinces and social effects on the characters, and especially of her protagonists who are mainly women. Years prior to Butler's philosophical account of this question, Mexican author Inés Arredondo had given an account of this in her fictional account of the subject in a short story titled "Canción de cuna" [Lullaby], published in 1965.

Born in 1928 in Culiacán of the Mexican state of Sinaloa, she died in 1989 in Mexico City. During her life she published a few books of short stories and some essays. Despite this relatively modest number of published edited works, Arredondo is considered one of the best Mexican writers; greater recognition of her work will surely follow. In Arredondo's short stories and essays we gain insight into a stark world in which the desire to be loved, seen and heard is the premise upon which our identities are built and by which their contours are marked. For our purposes here, I offer a reading of her short story "Canción de cuna" first published in the collection titled *La señal* [The sign] (1965). She published three other short story collections in her lifetime: *Río subterráneo* (1979) [Subterranean River], *Opus 123* (1983) and *Los espejos* [Mirrors] (1988). These are collected in two editions of her completed works (1988 and 1991, first and second editions respectively).

MUSIC AND THE IDENTITY-FORMATION IN ARREDONDO'S LULLABY

"Canción de cuna" (Arredondo, 1991, 49–57) is the seventh work of prose in her first book, a collection of 14 short stories. The purpose of the access created by music generates an approximation to emotional anguish experienced by the female protagonist. The fragmentation of the subject in the story, the musical action upon which that is symbolized and subsequently resolved, and the desire to recuperate the self-mediated by a musical experience through a remembrance of the past and a negation of the self, are three aspects we see at play in this text. In it the reader must grapple with references to music to awaken dimensions in the text associated with memories of previous musical experiences, and thus is a recalled sonorous experience, rather than a direct one, and is ambiguous, as this will be different for each receptor of the text. This openness further destabilizes the allusion to the musical meaning in the story.

Jean-Jacques Nattiez distinguishes music from other forms of communication, such as verbal language, proposing that all music remains a virtual object, in a state of "unconsummated symbol" (129). For this reason,

> music is not a narrative, but an incitement to make a narrative, to comment, to analyze. We could never overemphasize the difference between music, and music as the object of metalanguages to which it gives rise. Only thus can we start to outline its symbolic functioning. (128–29)

The potentiality of meaning inherent in music in general is also a factor for the reading of meaning in Arredondo's story. In particular as well are the socio-cultural references to a shared community and to intertextualities resident of those webs of signification and cultural memory. Arredondo's story places its focus from the title on the lullaby, in which the "cancion de cuna" premises the musical experience of infancy and the relationship to the mother in the formation of the subject.

The structure of the text places the fragmentation of personal relationships and feminine identity front and center. In the final outcome these resort to music that brings stability along at least one of the familial lineages, the matrilineal. The protagonist, a woman of 52 years, gathers her five adult children and 12 grandchildren to inform them that she is pregnant. After naming each of her sons and daughters and their children by name, the protagonist, who remains nameless throughout the story, emphasizes that she has accomplished her familial mission as mother and grandmother, and now wishes to have another child. She hopes they share her joy. Her children's shock upon receiving the news makes the protagonist defensive, and she attacks them verbally for judging the fatherless child she will bear. This beginning to the story reveals the psychological origins of the dichotomy between madness of "el embarazo imaginario" (49) or the imagined pregnancy, and sickness or the "pólipo uterino" (49), uterine polyp, within which a new birth and reconstitution of the lost fragments of the subject will surface in the rest of the narration.

The bipartite narrative structure reflects this by presenting two narrative voices—in the first and third person—in separate and ambiguous temporal spaces, which together weave the new identity based on the movement between them. The first person narration serves as the grounding frame of the field of action, while the third person flashbacks are presented in non-linear fashion, disconcerting the reader at times. This movement or connection in the story told is ushered in by musical memory. The intercalation of musical fragments, song refrains, and pieces of verses, together crystallize the codes which are deciphered by a listener who has access to all these meanings: interestingly it will be a male doctor, who will do so. In addition the reader contends with the presence of German verses located within a Spanish-language text.

The first segment, and main frame of the narration is that of the mother-grandmother now turned expectant woman only, who is treated for this madness/sickness by a Dr. Wasserman, an old friend of her family's. The second level of narration appears intermittently in the voice of Erika, whose "banal situation," as Fabienne Bradu describes it, "as an adolescent girl who gave birth in secret to a baby girl which she would pass off as her sister, within the family and in society's eyes"[1] (Bradu 40). While in a solitary space, awaiting the birth of the baby, Erika plays her guitar and sings. According to Bradu, this narrative structure reproduces the "cyclical loneliness of feminine life and the over-determination of matriarchal line" (40). The main narrative voice of the woman is told using the past tense, while those moments depicting Erika's expressions of anxiety vis-à-vis her maternity exist in a frozen present tense communicative space. Erika mentions frequently the sense of invasion she feels as the faceless and formless mass takes over her body and is the cause of her isolation. Images of her loneliness are evoked in the narrative descriptions of a desert landscape visible from her window. Her only company and physical solace is her guitar from which she produces original songs she composes while in this space of separation from the family and from the outside world.

SPATIAL AND MUSICAL ALLUSIONS

There are five segments in the story line that guide the interconnection among the two parallel temporal spaces. The musical references first appear in the second segment with the appearance of a character subsequently identified as Erika. Following the steps of the woman, a line of text from a song Erika was singing a German lullaby placed at the end of the third segment: *"als der stummen Eisamkeit / als der stummen Eisamkeit"* (Arredondo 53).

The Spanish translation of these verses provided by the narrative voice only near the end of the story, include the two cited above: "No one should find out / I will reveal it to no one / *except to the mute silence* [translation to English mine]. From those two verses in German, the narration jumps to the visit with "the psychiatrist, friend of the family" (53) [translation mine]. Here we learn that the family had decided that the best route to the woman's recovery was hypnosis so that she could sleep and rest. Dr. Wasserman appears here as the "old professor" (53) [translation

---

[1] All translations in the text from Spanish to English are mine. Those of the verses from German to Spanish were kindly provided by Prof. Alexandra Zimmerman, Wilfrid Laurier University, in 2005.

mine] who had known her parents, and when the woman has her visit with him, she is seen reclining with a bunch of grapes, "curving her lips" (53) and flirting with the doctor, as the narrator describes:

> Había algo en el movimiento de sus manos, en el modo de ladear de tiempo en tiempo la cabeza, de curvar los labios, que me hizo pensar en la coquetería gratuita que imagino en las mujeres de fin de siglo, de épocas pasadas que se han repetido en la historia, en que las mujeres han podido mantener centrada una esencia que no tiene nombre pero que en ese momento yo veía surgir en mi madre" (53).

> (There was something in the movement of her hands, the way she tilted her head back and forth, the curve of her lips, that made me think of the gratuitous fliratiouness that I imagine in women of the turn of the century, from ages past that have repeated in history, an essence women have been able to maintain that has no name but that in this moment I saw arise in my mother.)[2]

It is a "silent language" between the woman and the man. At this point in the story, the woman speaks with the doctor: "—De muy joven yo tocaba la guitarra…me gustaba. No he vuelto a probar. Me enseñó mi hermana Erika" (53). [From a very young age I played guitar…I liked it. I haven't tried again. My sister Erika taught me.]

The narrator, daughter of the protagonist, returns with the guitar they've had in the home for years without knowing that the woman could play: "Volví y el professor afinó el instrumento. Mi madre observaba atentamente al Viejo concentrado en su tarea. Por fin Wassermann la tendió la guitarra. Ella la recibió gentilmente y comenzó a tocar con toda facilidad, creo que sin recordar que hacia tantos años que no lo hacía. Luego, poco a poco, tarareo y cantó una canción de hacía treinta años, que yo le había escuchado muchas veces; una canción de moda en su juventud. Pero una vez unidos el canto y la guitarra aquello sonaba horriblemente mal. El profesor se levantó lentamente del asiento y se acercó a ella. Escuchó con mucha atención la guitarra, y de pronto, sobre la voz de ella comenzó a decir clara y firmemente: ""Hänschen klein geht allein / in die weite Welt hinein" (55) [*Johnny walks alone in the distant world.*]
The submerged memory had remained as tacit knowledge, as a subconscious truth until it could be revealed safely. The receptive safety of the doctor who listens, and who is able to decode the double sounding of the truth—the outward social layer known by all but serving as a mask to protect the family, and the hidden truth in the fifth string of the guitar playing of the girl's desire to be heard and accepted for who she is.

By playing the guitar, the protagonist recreates the hidden story of her mother, Erika. The flashbacks to Erika's story reveal the truth to readers bit by bit, and are accompanined to spatial references that indicate the temporal shifts. We come to

---

[2] All translations from Spanish to English from the original short story by Arrendondo are mine.

understand what is happening by inferring that the pains Erika experiences are actually those of pregnancy: "Y el vaivén secreto comienza: la muchacha se inclina y espía la próxima ola que la hará presentir de nuevo el oscuro universo del principio, y en tanto, pensando en el que lucha por ser, por salir, sus dedos modulan una antigua melodía luminosa, y ella murmura las palabras con infinita piedad, aunque las palabras no sirvan: *"Was ich in Gedanken küsse"* (53) [And the ebb and flow begins: the girl leans forward and senses the next wave that will make her feel the dark universe of the beginning, and meanwhile, thinking about who is struggling to be, to come out, her fingers modulate the luminous ancient melody, and she murmurs the words with infinite piety, even though the words don't serve any purpose: *What I kiss in my thoughts*]. She herself finds the process mysterious while she is living it as a teenager. Yet the song sustains her throughout the process. Not the words; language is insufficient as protection against fear. The music of the ancient song and the sounds she makes with it. The aliteration of the bilabial m's and n's repeated in the above sentence serve to echo the soothing sounds of the music, indeed its maternal sounds, its lullaby quality. Seen through her eyes, the sections of the narrative that return to the past heighten the sense of loneliness, fear and sadness experienced by the adolescent Erika:

> Sigue vigilando el latido subterráneo, se queda suspensa al borde del mundo del terror y del milagro, con todos los sentidos centrados en la cavidad que está en su cuerpo pero no es suya: la caverna sin luz en que están encerrados todos los signos pero donde nada tiene todavía sentido. El informe nada y se asemeja a otros informes que pasan a su lado, su boca redonda chupa al azar lo que puede, en el vertiginoso paso, tan parecido a lo inmóvil, del tiempo virgen, el que nadie contó. / Como si quisiera ocultar o conducir la lucha que le parece espera, sigue susurrando en su lengua, la lengua en que le hablo su madre, la canción que brota de la guitarra y en la que ella no piensa. (Arredondo 53)

> (She keeps monitoring the subterranean beating, suspended at the edge of the world of terror and miracle, with all her senses focused on the hollow space in her body though it doesn't belong to her; the cavern without light which encloses all signs but in which nothing yet has meaning. The unformed swims and seems like other unformed ones that pass alongside, with his round mouth randomly sucking what he can, along a vertiginous path, so still, as if belonging to virgin time, and what no one ever talked about. / As if she wanted to hide or manage the battle like constant waiting, she continues to whisper in the language her mother spoke, the song that emerges from the guitar and in which she does not have to think.)

The interior space of the cloistered room in which Erika is hidden during her pregnancy is contrasted by the description by the third person narrative voice of what is seen outside Erika's window:

> Sobre la llanura inmensa la paja amarillenta se eriza bajo la lluvia. El día gris extiende su tiempo sin esperanza. Ayer y mañana fueron y serán iguales, sin otra cosa que lluvia y frío; barridos interminablemente por el viento que se lleva todo color, toda voz, cualquier insinuación de alegría. (Arredondo 51)

> (Upon the vast plain the yellow hay stands under the rain. The grey day spreads its time hopelessly. Yesterday and today were and will be the same, nothing but rainy and chilly; endlessly swept by the wind that takes away all colour, all voice, any hint of joy.)

The vastness and emptiness of the plains serve to provide a visual escape for Erika, yet at the same time echo the loneliness and emptiness that she feels. Her emotionl state and her physical isolation are equally reflected in the barren landscape that she sees from her bedroom. The memory of the separation, thus, has taken hold of the perceived past recalled by a first-person narrator who presents the story obliquely through the persepctive of her grandmother (Erika) and her mother (the nameless protagonist). Interestingly, the pesistence of formlessness is also implied in the absence of the sujective power of the female protagonist, who remains nameless through the story. The gestures of the body and the sounds and sights become more real than communication between the family members. In the subsequent paragraph the narration highlights the failure of words to articulate Erika's experience:

> La soledad entra por la alta ventana. A pesar de los vidrios la habitación es helada, húmeda, y el viento, sitiando, aislando, hace sentir que se está dentro de una torre, la única en una orilla deshabitada del mundo, donde resulta inútil ensayar palabras, tener recuerdos. El viento y la lluvia seguirán azotando hasta borrar los rastros humanos" (Arredondo 51).

> (Solitude enters through the high window. Despite the glass the room is freezing, humid, and the wind, beseiging, isolating, makes it feel like being inside a tower, the only one on the uninhabited edge of the world, where it's pointless to try to speak any words, or to remember. The wind and the rain will continue flogging until all human traces are gone.)

The feminine subject disappears amidst the vastness of the surrounding spaces. The reflection of the world reveals nothing about her, no trace of her life. Until the music of the guitar appears in the subsequent paragraphs of the story (Arrendondo 51-52). Nevertheless, despite her presence reaffirmed throught the sound of singing and playing the stringed instrument in these sections, time seems to stand still: "El tiempo y el espacio ilimitados, muertos, y la muchacha a la deriva en ellos, sin otro sostén que el dedo sobre la cuerda y el sonido aislado. Así, eternamente" (51). She is ignorant of the cause of the limbo in which she lives, and is surprised the sensations of her body:

Pero un día, una tarde igual a otras, las manos de la muchacha se crispan y la guitarra cae al suelo. Un grito y el terror rompen la repetición helada. El sinsentido se corporiza y violenta el orden de la muerte: en el vientre de la niña un ser extraño se ha desperezado. Rasca y mueve las entrañas ciegamente. Ella siente la satisfacción bestial del informe ser que la habita sin conciencia; la lejanía insalvable en que busca acomodo, placer; estos pequeños saltos de reptil con que la hace ajena a sí misma. (Arredondo 52)

(But one day, one afternoon like any other, the hands of the girl twitch and the guitar falls to the ground. A scream and terror break the freezing recurrence. The pointlessness materializes and invades death's order: in the belly of the girl a strange being has awakened. It scratches and moves the entrails blindly. She feels the beastly satisfaction of the formless being that inhabits her without awareness; the insurmountable distance in which it seeks comfort, pleasure; this small reptilian leaps which disconnects her from herself.)

RECOVERING MEMORY THROUGH DIGITAL PERFORMANCE

The woman's sense of self and determination of identity, thus, required the male gaze and dialogue with this birthing male other in order to feel reconstituted as a subject within the norms of the society. It is interesting to note that this occurs in this story with a German doctor, of the same generation of the protagonist, and not with a Mexican male, who would have been her biological father. Thus what she seeks is not a father figure, but rather a mate, or an equal voice, to balance the birthing of her self. She has awakened the truth by instilling it in her musical memory for so many years. Having heard her mother perform the song to her as a child, indeed both as children, one the mother and the other the daughter, the intimaye event is preserved in the original composition by the former: "*als der stummen Eisamkeit*" (2x) (Arredondo 55); "*que (a) la muda soledad*" (55) ["*Einsamkeit*" is later translated in the text into Spanish, "*soledad*" (Arredondo 56)]. The cursive marks for the readers a sense of the song as sung, as separate from the speaking voice. The event is private and yet serves to witness the silencing of the identity of the daughter.

The way in which this takes place also elucidates the quality of subconscious materiality nascent from the body in the definition of self and sexual identity. The playing of the guitar, with the emphasis on the reclination of the body giving way to the touch of the fingers on the strings, awakens the mysterious language of the two melodies which the protagonist plays on the instrument while she sings a song in German. The discovery of her ability to speak German, her mother tongue, is a fact which by virtue of the doctor's exclamation, reveals the hidden and taboo nature of this connection to the mother. As well, it amplifies the hitherto exclusion of the protagonist from the mother's original field of cultural reference, as she was born after the family had immigrated to Mexico. The placement of the popular songs in guitar music links the protagonist to her new cultural Hispanic space, thus integrating both the German and Hispanic elements into one musical body; it becomes the instrument for expressing a deeper, hidden truth. This revelation links both narrative spaces and allows the protagonist the possibility of "performing" her birth and artistically re-enacting herself.

"CANCIÓN DE CUNA" AND PERFORMATIVITY

It is precisely this: to remove the "stageliness" of performativity, return naturalness to it, as Butler suggests be done in her concept of sexuality. For Butler, "'performativity' is not a specialised [sic/z] phenomenon. That is, she calls acts 'performative' when they *constitute the natural* – always in terms of some specific 'thing' – although through discursively constrained, but nonetheless signifying, gestures and speech. Power thus operates at this conjunction between human activity and meaning, and it 'produces' in language what the language 'claims merely to represent' (Butler 1999 [1990]: 5; see also Butler 1997a: 2-3). The connection between moving into gesture and embodied activity on the one hand, with speech choices on the other, also implies that there is muchnon-verbal terrain through which the subject constitutes itself. The choices on how to articulate the verbal acts in conjunction to, or at times in contrast to, by subjugation or hiding elements of the self, through this performativity. We could later add to this perception of how the self mediates itself in social relations the role that the subconscious plays. Therefore by examining to what extent previous experiences of space and encounter of self-motived actions have been affected by factors that are perhaps not regulated by conscious decision-making practices. In this sense, the body sometimes knows or remembers experiences that are not necessarily completely rationalized or of which the subject is not fully conscious, at least in terms of the effects those past experiences have on present actions, feelings and perceptions. In these terms, music as a vehicle for memory and for non-verbally constructed meaning is present in the body.

Roland Barthes emphasizes the spatial predominance in the musical image in another study in *The Responsibility of Forms*, which is rooted in the body; he writes, "in music, a field of signifying and not a system of signs, the referent is unforgettable, for here the referent is the body" (308). As such, of the two spheres of interpreting the song, tonality (a language, by traversing the scale of tones) and beats, the second is more significant (309). For Barthes, "tonality can have an *accentual* function (it participates in the **paragrammatical** structure of the musical text). When the tonal system disappears…this function passes to another system, that of timbre. 'Timbrality' (the network of timbre colors) assures the body the entire richness of its 'beats' […]. It is then the 'beats' – sole structural elements of the musical text which constitute music's trans-historical continuity, whatever the system (itself perfectly historical) the beating body uses to produce utterance" (310).

Writing about Schumann, and his indications of movements, who connoted his texts in the vernacular, Barthes reads this "explosion of the mother tongue into the musical text [as] an important phenomenon. He writes in "Rasch" that "the explosion of the *Muttersprache* in musical writing is really the declared restoration of the body – as if, on the threshold of melody, the body discovered itself, assumed itself in the double depth of the beat and of language; as if, with regard to music, the mother tongue occupied the place of the *chora* (a notion adapted from Plato by Julia Kristeva): the indicating word is the receptable of *signifying*" (310). And in those indications in the mother tongue, Barthes says we read the body in that "they tell about the body" rather than metronomic movement (310). What is left to language is to piece together the effects of those surprise movements; first perceived by the body, and then represented in speech acts as if to mirror back the effects, the process of interpreting the interaction of the body in spatial reality requires work of retracing the steps performed.

EMBRACING THE GUITAR AS RECUPERATION OF SELF

In "Problèmes de linguistique général II" (1974), "Benveniste sets in opposition two realms of signification: the *semiotic*, an order of articulated signs each of which has a meaning (such as the natural language), and the *semantic*, an order of discourse no unit of which signifies in itself, although the ensemble is given a capacity for signifying. Music, Benveniste says, belongs to semantics (and not to semiotics); hence, Benveniste continues, music is a language which has a syntax but no semiotics" (311). As Barthes characteristically does, he then adds the element of desire, in which he believes music is steeped (312), provoking a change in logics (312): "it therefore relates to a semanalysis, or one might say to a second semiology, that of the body in a state of music; let the first semiology manage, if it can, with the system of notes, scales, tones, chords, and rhythms; what we want to perceive and to follow is the effervescence of the beats. / By music, we better understand the Text as signifying [*significance*]" (312). The body's truth has been saved through music, while the conscious self, the thinker who needed to navigate a social setting in which her lack of a father and the true nature of her birth to an unwed teenager, would have led to her being shunned, shamed and marginalized. It has taken three generations for the truth to be revealed, not only to others but also to herself. The journey initated by the presence in the body of the uterine polyp that mysteriously appeared in her mature age, when she was already a grandmother herself, is the stage during which the illegitimate daughter is released from her forgetfulness. The woman she had considered her mother, is in fact her grandmother; and Erika, whom she was raised to believe was her sister, is her mother. The final scene between the protagonist who has fallen ill in order to discover the truth of her existence and parentage occurs with her mother, Erika. On her deathbed, Erika confesses everything to her. Thus, initiating the journey back to the unconscious knowing. Music is the catalyst that simultaneously shields the truth in physical memory (the ways the song is remembered on the guitar without any conscious recollection of such knowing), and also releases the subject from the layers and years of lies. The language of the body has superseded verbal language. Its subtextual force has resided in the sound memory of the daughter cum grandmother.

It is interesting to note as well the use of the guitar as symbol. Its instrumentality is intimate. To play this instrument it must be embraced. Its presence in the scene of the protagonist (who remains nameless in the story) mirrors the way a child is nestled in a mother's arms. It is the main image at the cathartic point of the story in which the protagonist plays on the guitar the song that her mother would play to her in their shared hidden scapes behind closed doors in the family home. Inverting the roles, the protagonist takes the reins of her hidden story. Her capacity to do so rests on the encoding of the truth that her mother, Erika, has performed in the object of the song; one that is doubly voiced: one is a German nursery song, the other an original composition by Erika as an expression of her profound loneliess during her pregnancy. The silence of the family that ensues after the birth also denotes sadness to the song in its persistent cry to be heard beneath the surface communications of the family.

HER STORIES: SINGING THE LEGACY

The final paragraph of the short story by Arredondo emphasizes the cyclical nature of familial patterns. When one woman is released from social and patriarchal lies at the heart of the family identity, all are released as well.

> La canción de mi abuela y de mi madre me envuelve. Mi historia es diferente, mi hijo tiene padre, tendrá madre, pero ahora no somes ambos más que una masa informe que lucha. En el principio otra vez. Me inclino sobre mi vientre y escucho. Estamos solos. Y todo vuelve a comenzar. (Arredondo 57)

> (The song of my grandmother and mother envelop me. My story is different, my child will have a father, will have a mother, but now we are both nothing more that a formless mass that struggles. At the beginning once again. I lean over my belly and listen. We're alone. And everything begins again.)

The narrator is one of the protagonist's daughters, now an expectant mother herself, who ponders this story as one of empowerment for her child. Thus, storytelling and singing are intertwined in the narrative voice. Music as a subtext in women's writing becomes an emancipating force. It also returns to the beginning, an origin of spatial identity, at once formless and connected to the other. Maternity returns the mother to her concept of birth, reactivating the memory of her origin, expressed in this closing paragraphe of Arredondo's story given that "we are nothing more that a formless mass that struggles" (57). Uneasy with this state, both mother and child struggle to become free to each other and give birth to new life.

This section has traced the lineage of female subjects established through music, and its relationship to storytelling. It sits on the side of the voice of women as an antidote to familial storytelling that would seek to marginalize her truth; at the same time it recovers storytelling as a device for conveying the musical meaning of the bodies affected by recorded family histories. In our close reading of this short story by Mexican author Inés Arredondo, language, power and identity interact in a first-person narrative of a third-generation member of a German immigrant family in Mexico. The incorporation of songs in German and Spanish reveal the liberation available to the female subject through musical expression as it serves to release blocked memories and build connections to lost family ties.

Creation Sounds

CHAPTER 2

Poetic Bodies, Soundspaces and 'The World Wide Womb'

And in her body a music of griefless things shall weave
Savirtri

(R)E-POSITIONING POETIC BODIES IN GLOBAL/CIVIL WOR(L)D SYSTEMS

The fluctuating appraisal on the nature of reality has often been reflected in poetry as it moves beyond the spaces of established discourse, external physical space and the way we perceive the world through exegesis of the world-as-text. Reaching through language and its discourses and yet continually re-opening these as vehicles and organizers of meaning is a trait that distinguishes poetry from other genres; at its very heart, the play with meaning has a source that exceeds meaning and thus is beyond fixity, a harbinger of the ebbs and flows of history, the sciences of the mind, of affect and the human endeavours in the expression of culture and the political.

Chilean poets Malú Urriola, Nadia Prado and Cecilia Vicuña (the latter exiled to the UK in 1973 and based in New York since 1980), put in practice notions borne from Latin American concepts of reality, from the various iterations and flows of mappings and re-mappings at the level of the observable and of the aspects formerly hidden from human sight. In their collaborative project, *Poesía es +* (2002) [*Poetry is more*], Nadia Prado and Malú Urriola made sky waves when they recited their poems on megaphone [3], subverting and re-engaging with this well-known device for marketing ads, while riding in a hot-air balloon or flying banners of poetic verses on biplanes over historically-marked spaces of Santiago. Their urban interventions posited a poetic body in contrast to the lies beheld by the social eye and the amnesia instilled by a neo-liberal, post-dictatorial hold over Chilean public space.

Combining this with a reading of Cecilia Vicuña's visual and rhythmic word bodies in the travelling installations of raw wool, sound and performance her series of installations titled *Cloud-Net* (1999), I detect similar resonances with Kristeva's later

---

[3] In an article published in the *Writers' Yearbook 2014*, Kevin Kaiser argues that the current "rules of marketing" are being re-written, as the importance of building relationships with smaller sets of audiences replaces older forms of practice for securing market share in a given financial arena. He advises contemporary authors that, in order "to get notices and make your own waves" (35), "Learn how a little creative thinking can take you a long way" (35). His reasoning stems from the view that "many publishers and authors see online spaces and social media as just another megaphone, much like the ad companies did when banner ads were invented. They want 'impressions,' not relationships. That's how the vast majority of marketers think. But which are you looking for?" (Kaiser 37).

incarnations in her interpretation of the concept of the "chora" as a process of signification, whereby material space opens towards new practices of revolt. In both *Poesía es +* and *Cloud-Net* the artists posit a way for the sensory reception of spaces in movement (made "dynamic" by a constant flow of individual interactions that overlap and multiply into greater levels of collective effects); their multiple meanings grow as they become sites associated with successive generations of specific memory constructions and the shared perception and agreement of these. In this chapter I explore how Prado, Urriola and Vicuña's poetic urban interventions reveal the evolving perception of reality in terms of the latest concepts related to quantum physics and its considerations of physical space. It also questions the psychology of space in relation to the body's situation and its capacity to hold non-verbal meanings that render the space-time continuum more complex in the consideration of inter-subjectivity and world making.

By reinterpreting the apparent "dynamism" of city spaces as a continual rebirthing process, a recurrence to the spaces of *chora* undoes the stagnancy and devolution of otherwise imposed death cycles. In this way, these poets reveal the nature of quantum reality and its transformative capacities for questioning contemporary notions of realism in order to posit openness to connections beyond material appearances as permanent but rather malleable cycles that require input from a collective agreement; as such, therefore, they can be undone and re-made, albeit via a process that is complex and unpredictable, linking both material and apparently immaterial structuring systems.

Notwithstanding the magnitude and confluence of many diverse cultures, tendencies and shifts that point to the now known concept of what it means to be Latin American, and of the ideological divides of the Americas that cross national boundaries, these poets manifest in their texts that "space is the primary thing and matter only secondary" (Einstein, 1930: 1). For Ervin László, Hungarian philosopher of science,

> Matter, in the last analysis is a bound form of energy, and space and time are an integral dynamic element, interacting with matter and energy in all its forms. This 'deep basement' of the universe is variously called quantum vacuum, unified vacuum, physical spacetime, hyperspace, or nuether. Despite these abstruse terms, its existence is not merely theoretical and…it is not a vacuum and not just a space. It is an energy—an information-filled 'cosmic plenum,' the womb of all that exists, and the background of all that happens. (2008, 88)

To exhibit a true depiction of reality is to examine the deeper levels of interaction of energy in which space is unbound by matter. By making evident that there is more than the eye can see, and yet by putting into the forefront that what the eye sees can lie, these poets attempt to reveal a reality that is continually in the making at a deeper level in the "cosmic plenum" or "deep basement" as per László's depiction.

The Kristevan definition of the *chora* operative here is that which has persisted in the work of the French literary theorist, despite having undergone several revisions and the effects of several critiques, and those even of Kristeva hereself, for its supposed over-emphasis on the "essentialized feminine" or, as Anna Smith argued, its "failure" to develop "a structure that would mediate between semiotic and symbolic so that neither entropy nor a deadly abstraction prevails" (cited in Magroni 92). Kristeva's focus takes after Plato's *Timeus* in some regards, such as its emphasis on the "third" option, while departing significantly in others (see Magroni 2001; Beaujour 1975; Walker 1998). If we, however, place the persistence of the *chora* in her work, especially in the definitions afforded in *Revolution in Poetic Language*, and her updates afterward, as Magroni has noted, Kristeva's "aim is to turn the 'problem,' the 'aporia' of this relation [that of the 'demonic' and the social, desire and the Law, material production and representation] into an enabling passage, tracing in it the possibility of a transformative *practice* that opens up the speaking subject as much as law and society to what comes from the 'outside' (outside the self, logos, the organized body-politic)" (Magroni 92). According to Magroni's reading of Kristeva, "her exploration of a space of ambiguous relationality in the context of which the possibility of our transcendence to the 'demonic' lies (to paraphrase Stephen Watson) 'less beyond us' than 'in–between' constitutes, perhaps, her greatest contribution as a postmodern thinker" (Magroni 93–94). Yet this posits another complexity that is the situatedness of the body and its remembrances. I link this here with the newest advances in physics, particularly to draw on the discovery of what constitutes reality at the level of quarks in relation to matter; this allows us to tease out the paradoxes of the Kristevan approach to the *chora*. Moreover, I propose the art events by Prado, Urriola and Vicuña as praxis of this approach.

Poetry's textually supported capacity for self-creative agency to empower individually within a collective environment is found in both *Poesía es +* and *Cloud-Net*. By text, however, we are not referring only to the surface upon which the art rests, nor equating it solely to visible matter, but in terms of the forces which are in relation to the sensed underlying energy base (at the intersection of wave/particle observational theories), for the most part unseen, except at times through its effects. In their art actions, Prado, Urriola and Vicuña posit a way for the sensory reception of the spaces that urges a reinterpretation of the "dynamism" of collective spaces. The predominance of the urban center in this view, multi-layered in its sites of memory, stems from the concentrated historically driven and coincidental interaction and appearance of our bodies in these places as intimate urban collectives. They are intimate in the sense of being released from or reduced to the spectral or the superficially specular level of appearance; instead the focus radiates from the interiority of the body, which is both spatially and non-spatially defined at once. These poets reveal the evolving perception of reality in terms of the latest concepts related to quantum physics and its considerations of physical space. Viewed in conjunction with what Butler has proposed for the political in the performativity of the body in gender studies, this is not in contradiction to what Kristeva has explored from the perspective of the generative capacity of creative expression, as we shall see further on in the particular acts of poetry which manifest transformative capacities for reimagining contemporary notions of realism.

QUARKS AND DEFINING HISTORICAL BODIES

Since the 1960s with the discover of quarks, and more recently with the confirmation of the Higgs Boson (2008-2012), scientists can agree in what ways vast inner spaces are rendered perceptible as outer structures. Scaled depending on our perspective, the potential for linkages across space-time fields can be unhinged from their former appearances depending on the tools and viewpoints used for their observation.

In their 2002 collaborative project, *Poesía es +* [Poetry is + (More)], Urriola and Prado question previous definitions of "realism" in relation to the effects of normative language on the body politic. Positioning their work in air spaces above the Chilean capital city, they made waves in public air space with their poetic urban interventions. From this work was borne a poetic language whose objective was to recapture a lost freedom belonging to language in its capacity to comment on history, memory and the present re-working of the reality ascribed to a space in the very moment of its appearance. By reciting their poetry via megaphone, their work represented a dual critique of the nature of the intersections of individuals in a collective, public space.

Part of this critique is a reconsideration of neoliberal tolos of commerce and their symbolism for receptive practises that take into account these familiar forms of social communication and consumption of information. In a recent article published in the *Writers' Yearbook 2014*, Kevin Kaiser argues that the current "rules of marketing" are being re-written, as the importance of building relationships with smaller sets of audiences replaces older forms of practice for securing market share in a given financial arena. He advises contemporary authors that, in order "to get noticed and make your own waves" (35), they must "learn how a little creative thinking can take you a long way" (35). His reasoning stems from the view that "many publishers and authors see online spaces and social media as just another megaphone, much like the ad companies did when banner ads were invented. They want 'impressions,' not relationships. That's how the vast majority of marketers think. But which are you looking for?" (37). Thus, in what way did Prado and Urriola wish to invoke this impression via an outmoded form of advertisement, taken over and used for a poetic expression of discontent via the present?

Voicing their poems while riding in a balloon over historically marked spaces of Santiago, in one part of their series of performances, they had to be close enough to the streets to be heard and seen physically. In this way, they unhinged a monolithic interpretation of each public space to reveal hidden underlying assumptions. The method they chose also subverted the stability of neoliberal marketing techniques of a past era. By moving outside the confines of the book for all of these "urban interventions" and placing their work in spaces usually employed by advertising and publicity, privelging sound and gesture, these Chilean poets intervened poetically and placed their bodies and their texts before the "social eye" (quoted in Chávez 2003; translation mine) on and over locations marred by historical atrocity and forgetfulness (such as the National Stadium, ex-center of repression and torture during the first years of the military dictatorship, and the Puerto de San Antonio, severely marked by unemployment). Among their stated intentions is that of recovering the precariousness of living language as an alternative to the stagnancy of forgetfulness and the numbing terror of warfare. As Prado explains, "we wanted to bring the social eye closer to the poetic body and give a different possibility for appearing, as it moves us to an alternative space from that of the written support of a book" (in Chávez 2003; translation mine).

Combining this with a reading of Vicuña's art installations and visual/rhythmic word *bodies* in *Cloud-Net* (1999), there are resonances with Kristeva's proposition of the potential for revolt. The semiotic *chora* is the source of language's outskirts. It is a heterogeneous and productive non-space that extends beyond and between individual bodily form. As such it can contain new forms of speech, and is attributable to the creative aspect of language. Although the *chora* is situated by Kristeva in the pre-Oedipal stage, it can still appear as pulsations and rhythmic interventions in language to press upon and produce meaning effects that are beyond the limitations of a Lacanian male symbolic order, to reach into a differently gestated "female symbolic order" (Kristeva 1999 and 2002; Irigaray [1985] 2002).

The Kristevan *chora* serves to understand the creative process and the participation of our bodies as markers of memory. The *chora* is a type of articulation capable of resisting entrapment in previous notions of meaning. Rhythmic and sensory it becomes visible only as an effect on the body and its chosen responses to these sounds and sensations. As such, it can be encapsulated in linguistic signs only after the body has perceived it more directly. As it is neither a sign nor a position, but rather "a 'wholly provisional articulation that is essentially mobile and constituted of movements and their ephemeral stases, … [it] only admits analogy with vocal or kinetic rhythm" (Kristeva cited in Moi, 1985, 161). In this sense the poetry and the visual imagery we find in Vicuña resonate with the underlying pulsating nature of the Kristevan *chora* and its potentiality, as the *chora* represents the "wavelike variation" (93) described by László in relation to the functioning of quarks. Therefore, a site of engagement and observation must be pinpointed in order to determine the meaning of its reality.

POETRY AND THE CITY

For the most part, the vocal expression in the *poetry art actions* by Prado and Urriola is located in urban spaces. The process continuously returns to a downtown city centre, albeit that the trajectory often originates at the outskirts. Extrapolated to the historical perspective on dictatorship and its aftermath, the downtown/outskirts binary creates a larger outflow of meaning and its potential reversals, such as that of here/there in the experiences of exile, or the here/now versus the before/then dynamic of recovering memory across generations. The relation to centers of power is also playing on distance to agency. Defined from the space of the urb ("de la urbe," Rodríguez Saavedra and Chandía Fica 3), it implies a return from the peripheral "suburb," a term which originated in 1965-70, and which then is urbanized by the removal of the prefix, that is, it is a "backformation from suburb," according to *Random House Dictionary* (2014). By leaving the outskirts to come back to the urb, it becomes a focalized space up for negotiation in the two types of poetic art actions (*Poesía es +*, as we are discussing here, and *Cloud-net,* which we will examine subsequently). Sergio Rodríguez Saavedra and Bernardo Chandía Fica discuss the presence in recent

Chilean writing of the figure of "la urbe" in an essay titled, "Intimidad Urbana: Huellas de los Últimos Poetas del Siglo Veinte" ["Urban Intimacy: Footprints of the Last Poets of the Twentieth Century" [translation mine], wherein the *urb* is the contemporary ritual of belonging:

> **la lengua madre**, la norma, la institución dejan de ser el paradigma y el dogma de toda inscripción y de todo significado textual... lo decisivo de su singularidad consiste en su gesto tribal, escénico, urbano y bárbaro, infinitamente menos libresco y revisteril que las anteriores generaciones poéticas...Carecen de toda hermandad, de toda solidaridad beata, de capilla o grupo; carecen en definitiva, de todo culto a alguien, siendo su único rito la ciudad, la urbe, ciertas zonas y lugares de origen y de pérdida. (Rodíguez Saavdera and Chandía Fica 3).

> **the mother tongue** [emphasis mine], the norm, the institution are no longer the paradigm or the dogma of all inscription, or of all textual signification...its decisive singularity is constituted in a tribal, scenic, urban and barbarous gesture, infinitely less bookish and magazine-ish than previous generations of poets... They lack all brotherhood, all benign solidarity, of belief or group; they lack in effect, all cult to someone, their only rite the city, the urb, certain zones and places of origin and of loss. [my translation; emphases above in bold are also mine]

Two aspects are highlilghted here: (1) urbanity is recovered as a symbol of traversing to and from an energy source that is outside and nowhere, while it simultaneously appears anywhere determined by its relational force. [In the texts mentioned above, it acts as a textual referent whereby the city is the symbolic site of deprivation (solitude, alienation, loss]; (2) a return to the gestural and oral expression, or the oral nature of language that is beyond inscription, envelops a signalling of the "chora" in relation to the linguistic law. Belonging becomes about proximity and not pertaining to abstract constructions of socio-historical identity. By being selected for the art actions the city also becomes a crucial site of collective negotiation and future (ex)change of subjectivity and of choice.

    A return to a creative language within that space, anchored in the urban site, seeks to re-master a cycle of return to self and to relatedness. By not negating the site of what was previous lost through trauma (in the case of military or political oppression in capital cities of South and Central America during the second half of the twentieth century) and by recognizing the historical weight of each location, what is recuperated from a former stance of victimhood is the ability to articulate something within the very place of the former *dispossession* (Butler and Athanasiou 2014). The newly repositioned poetic body in the site of recovered memory becomes instead an agent of regeneration. Preceeding this is a necessary filtration through the dynamic creative movement createdvy the poets reciting live their poems via megaphone during visual/aerial performance in flight over each cityscape selected for the events.

According to the poetry in print thrown as leaflets from the airborne vessels of performativity, Urriola and Prado's collaborative four-part multimodal poetic intervention in urban spaces proposed a type of "Desrealismo" [Unrealism].

For the making of their flying text, Urriola and Prado conceived of a series of art actions that took place in a post-9/11 world (on both counts: Chilean and North American). Each of their "urban interventions" (2002), pre-announced via website[i], signaled a specific historical site for the poetic actions that took place over the Chilean capital's landscape. There were four art acts spanning over a week in October of 2002:

> I. The public performances began on October 9 at 8:00 p.m. with a reading on megaphone from a hot air balloon over Plaza Italia, in the center of Santiago.
> II. On October 11, at 1:00 p.m., a small aircraft flew over San Cristóbal Hill's Forest Park with a banner read, "¿Y si la jaula estuviera siempre abierta?" (And if the cage were always open?)[4].
> III. For the third *intervención*, on October 12, the poets took a two-hour hot air balloon ride over the economically-depressed fishing port of San Antonio, with a hanging banner stating that "Los ojos son libres " [Our eyes are free].
> IV. The final of the four acts took place on October 15, beginning at 10:00 a.m., over the *Estadio Nacional*, known to have been a site of torture and disappearances during military rule under Pinochet. Their poems were recited on loudspeaker from a balloon as it hovered above the stadium, creating a contextually bound metaphor in defense of freedom, yet also suggesting a critical revision of "the impostures of the present" (2002).

The activities were filmed and photographed and subsequently exhibited as a whole in the cultural space of *Galpón 7*, Santiago, Chile on December 11, 2002.

Similar to other poets working in Chile in the post-dictatorial context, Prado and Urriola were encouraged by "the return to democracy in 1990, for they had awaited it many years under a system which used fear and death as political weapons. The year 1990 supposed the return of individual, social, political liberties, in effect the publicity campaigns spoke of the coming of happiness for all people" (Original text: "sintieron ilusión con el regreso de la democracia el año 90, pues la estuvieron esperando largos años bajo un sistema que usaba el miedo y la muerte como herramienta política. Ese año, 1990, suponía el regreso de las libertades individuales, sociales, políticas, de hecho las campañas publicitarias hablaban del advenimiento de la alegría para toda la gente.") (Rodríguez Saavedra Chandía Fica 4). For a compelling look at the political process carved out from the seemingly overwhelming

---

[4] All translations of Prado and Urriola's poems and interview scripts are mine, from the original Spanish, unless otherwise specified.

circumstances of the 1980s by the Chilean Left and other members of the population who wished to be liberated from the Pinochet government's oppression, see the film *NO* (2012) about the campaign of "No + (mas) [No + more]". The title of the work, *Poesía es +* alludes to this antecent. Evident is the paradox in the negative/positive affirmation of the 1988 plebiscite vote and the use of publicity campaign strategies turned instead as a tool for alternative free political and social expression.

The historical processes and political memory of victory inherent in the plus sign that became emblematic of that "no" vote to the Pinchot regime, and a "yes" vote for a positive alternative future is encapsulated in the sign that appears in the title of Prado and Urriola's *Poesía es +*, as a possible reply to what that "yea" vote would mean. Vicuña's work was also initiated under this thrust of *NO,* as founder and member of *Tribu No,* Santiago, 1967, and of Artists for Democracy, London, 1974. Yet she participated in these changes from abroad, representing the diaspora of Chileans, as well as other Latin American citizens, displaced during dictatorial regimes.

It is relevant to point out that the "No +" campaign paved the way for revealing how neoliberal and financial techniques for market expansion could be used for purposes other than narrowly drawn market-driven objectives. It is also representative of a distancing from the communist forefathers. In this case, capital is not seen pejoratively, but is placed in perspective as a possible benefit under new rules. This complexity makes a departure from previous Situationists avant-garde art movements and theories (SI) with a complete disdain for capitalism a resolute and monolithic rejection of any market or publicity-based tool. On the contrary, the *NO +* campaign aimed to reclaim the space of individual property and wellbeing, without abandoning private property as a means to secure a more just and resolute common good. The generation of poets who grew up under the Pinochet regime, and who later matured in the circumstances that followed, manifests an apprehension and release of past political opposition tactics.

While the successful return to democracy in 1990 was a highlight of these liberating efforts, after having suffered the aftermath of their own "9/11" (Schild) which occurred in 1973, it was to be a release into a new international arena now riddled with other pressures. As Chandía Fica and Rodríguez Saavedra explain, the jubilation at having won the referendum of 1990 which ousted Pinochet from the government was in sharp contrast to the,

> contrastaba con las noticias internacionales que anunciaban el fin de las utopías, la real desaparación de la Unión Soviética, parte de las potencias económicas mundiales. En dichas circunstancias estos poetas optaron por la cautela, observaron los hechos internos y externos y definieron sus pautas de trabajo artístico en respuesta a lo que se venía: una globalización o 'nuevo orden mundial' que implicaba que todos éramos consumidores y consumidos simultáneamente, momento representado en la voz del conjunto musical Los Prisioneros (fenómeno discográfico del rock chileno la pasada época). (Rodríguez Saavedra and Chandía Fica 4-5).

international news announcing the end of utopias, the real disappearance of the Soviet Union, part of the economic world powers. In these circumstances the poets opted for caution, observing internal and external events and defined their standards of artistic work in response to what was coming: a globalization or 'new world order' which implied that we were all consumers and consumed simultaneously, a moment represented in the voice of the musical group The Prisoners (album phenomenon of Chilean rock from the past epoch). (4-5) [my translation]

These literary critics argue that the main thrust of those tendencies in new Chilean poetry display a belief that "la poesía es un arma cargada de futuro" [poetry is a weapon loaded with the future] (8). The underlying theme, especially in what we observe in the works of Prado, Urriola and Vicuña is engagement for positive change.

In a comparable way to *Poesía es +,* Vicuña's work highlights the bridge between the mobile and living speech of the socialized body that intervenes artistically in urban spaces to question our shared assumptions of political alliances and disalliances, collective memories and official historical forgetting. Drawing out these threads in her various moving installations, such as in *Cloud-Net*, Vicuña's art acts and publications are an interesting counterpoint to the four urban interventions by Prado and Urriola on the way poetic signifiers can be rethought and remade in each site where the body appears to other bodies. *Cloud-Net* is mobile, transitional through space, as it appears in the streets or in various galleries, or in lectures-performances. It is also laden with the constructing of a "tribal" subjectivity (Sepúlveda 115-18), alongside the theme of memory and the role of spoken poetry and threads or pieces of refuse, which serve as a contra-canonical means to recover lost fragments of repressed speech (Sepúlveda 125-26), or defend that which is for the most part unseen or unheard in prevailing discourse.

In another of Vicuña works, *Spit Temple*, she clarifies this "ethics" of the poetic act that she is after, and reiterates that the "semilla es la memoria" [the seed is memory] (2012). We read in this collection of poems that: "Charles / Olson / said / memory is the future / because you will / remember in future tense / you will remember / whatever you did / and others did / and others will do / that is the change / think think / of / the killers / a desperate call for connection / think of / their / memory / think of their memory" (2012, 194-195). These interactions highlight the audible and the visible produced in spaces outside the confines of the book and of enclosed reading spaces in ways that reposition the role of the poetry.

Poesía es + is a challenge to overly determined assumptions of realism and prevailing uses of visual imagery and language that succumb to utilitarian, market-driven views. It positions poetry as an alternative to the neoliberal reality of consumerism and econonism, and as a challenge to hegemonic readings of historical events, becoming more suggestive in concert with other counter-hegemonic Gramscian projects. Alice Nelson has described the attempt of this work to resituate the social subject to provoke a critical revisioning of its condition within the city setting: "Not only have both bodies and the urban landscape become regulated in service of economic utility, but also the ability to negotiate social demands increasingly has become framed within the technical terms of neoliberal policies and norms, which Verónica Schild calls the 'dominant grammar' functionally defining self and society in Chile today" (Schild 2003, cited in Nelson 202).

At the same time, the immediacy of the project finds passersby where they are, in an attempt to awaken a personal stake in the desire to restore civil society and invoke latent common values based on cultural production's political agency, as grassroots actions had done in earlier decades. For Nelson, "two issues seem crucial here: first, that since 1990 the conflictual aspects of historical memory and debate have been defused within Chile's institutional democracy, which has tended to repress its own contradictions in a seamless official discourse based on consensus and reconciliation; and second, that the technologies of publicity and commercial discourse have only abetted that process, reducing social exchange to a kind of eternal present based on production and consumption" (202). In Poesía es + [Poetry is + (More)], the connection between language, image and bodies perceiving reality in their project moves the poetic text into various spheres at once, to create a tension with what we normally would assign as meaning there. The cycle of texts that move from the hot air balloons (twice in flight and once statically anchored at the National Stadium, and also in one biplane flight over the city of Santiago) are repeated in print through the use of handbills thrown from the airborne vessels, and as actions caught on photographic image, to be reproduced on internet sites and a subsequent book published in 2004.

The fourth intervention questions our notions of reality most directly. While the balloon held sway for a day over the stadium by displaying a vertical banner with the word "Memoria" from its basket, the poets distributed handbills printed with a poem titled "Cupón de Suscripción al desrealismo" (Coupon for Subscribing to Unrealism). The texts asked passersby questions such as "Do you believe that Reality exists? / Do you believe that Reality is real? ... Really you believe, think, feel, smell, / observe, hear, touch Reality? Do you believe that you are real? Or does Reality leave you without action? Are you still you? **Poetry is +**." The emphasis in bold from the original text highlights the potential to signify expressed materially in the artistic gesture. The movements along a vertical axis (the need to gaze upward at the poets reading aloud and to look downward to receive and read the handbills) also questions poetry's role in quotidian reality, surprising the receptors with its immediacy and situationality[5].

BIRTHING THROUGH POETIC LANGUAGE

Hot air balloons ascend, they rise; our gaze follows them as they move upwards in air, against whatever sky-scape they cross. It is also their slow movements that distinguish

---

[5] It would be interesting to compare this to the views of Situationists of the 1950s to early 1970s, specifically in terms of "psychogeography," although the poets discussed here do not make reference to the Situationists in their discussion about their works.

them from other aircraft, as does their lower level flights, closer to the ground and whose contours are more evident to the sights of onlookers. Not only do they represent human technology and its advances—as the first type of free-form flight, achieved in 1782—but they also represent a spirit of invention, a desire for freedom from physical constraints. At the same time, in a world oversaturated with advertisement, companies looking for ways to attract the attention of potential clients use this cost-effective method. They need to present it in a way that "the leisure-conscious and ad-hardened consumers can't help but notice" (Munro 22). Munro (1985) has noted that for the First of America Bank, it costs about $500 per event to operate a hot-air balloon. This amount represents a small percentage of the bank's advertising budget (22). To have taken flight in vehicles normally used, especially in the 1980s (Hellauer; Newman), for advertising purposes serves as a metaphor of questioning what it means, whether as resistance against consumerism, or as commentary about, the role of poetry, and the arts in general, in the public domain when linked in this way.

The shape of the balloon as metaphor of the reproductive cycle of the womb that produces objects for sale, or the "mechanics of reproduction" (Foucault 1990, 61) is also not lost here. Beyond the "machinery" metaphors, Newtonian style, what is most highlighted is the wind and air and heat forces that actually propel the vessel, not that rudimentary machinery that attempts to harness these. The forces at play are natural, not man-made. Each of these writers in her own way defines how the poetic word, as creative act, extricates itself from outside limitations or constraining notions of an imposed collective system; however, it does so in order to posit a different one, through questioning (as in the list of interrogatives distributed through the handbills) as an invitation to collaborate in the work.

Another work by Prado, *Carnal* (1998), speaks to this. In an interview about these poems, she says that poetry is a means of "turning language into flesh" (*Las últimas noticias).* The title of the work refers to the association of the word "carnal" to kinship; in some Latin American countries it symbolizes blood ties, flesh, but also "brother"-hood. She explained in this conversation that the term alludes to a sense of sisterhood that she feels with certain readers of her poetry. The tension between language and silence inherent in poetry is also evident, as it was in a previous book which had been published in 1992, *Simples placeres* [*Simple Pleasures*]. Prado admits that she had crossed over "into rage against a system that does not represent her and that language can only soothe her as a drug" (*Las últimas noticias*, 1998): "Nada alcanza, nada es suficiente, nada basta. Aunque todo se resista, aunque los barrotes sigan aquí, escribo y la tartamudez penetra la carne, la carne se niega, la carne es otra, otra, aparte de mí. La maldad se devora a sí / misma. Y el lenguaje emerge como un sedante". (Nothing reaches, nothing is enough, nothing lasts. Although / everything attempts to resist, / although the bars remain here / I write and / my stammering penetrates my skin, my flesh denies, my flesh is other, another part of me. Malice devours / itself. And language emerges like a sedative.[6]) This has external and internal

---

[6] Translation of these verses by Prado is mine from Spanish to English.

ramifications: "my stammering penetrates my skin…is other." The conflict from within the symbolic order, which Kristeva would argue post Lacan, is felt as an underlying pulsion. The comfort of the imposed order, even under the guise of economic stability and consumerist temptations, does not ring true any longer.

Instead of remaining in a pre-symbolic order, however, without access to any signification at all, the poetic voice in Prado's poetry, such as in *Carnal, Simples placeres* and *Poesía es +,* makes attempts to articulate the pulsion. Although the voice falters in Prado's text, the poem itself has fought against it remaining in complete silence. By expressing itself through stammering in *Simples placeres* cited above, the voice is heard, interpreted and transformed into gestural communication. The awareness that something seeks to be articulated, albeit laden with frustration, reveals the struggle for understanding in a shared space of encounter. What shapes that space of encounter takes a significant role in the meaning of the expression. Language as sedative becomes the antidote to the stammering chaos.

BEYOND FIGHT OR FLIGHT, POETRY IS

Returning to the seeds of memory, Prado and Urriola's works follow a trajectory of awakening latent meaning in the apparent environment. The discursive plays in *Poesía es +* flow also from previous generations of River Plate artistic phenomena such as the CADA poetic movement of the 1970s, with Damiela Eltit, Raúl Zurita, Eugenia Brito, Rodrigo Cá, among others, who participated in an experimental course on the work of Antonin Artaud. The work of recovering historical memory and uncovering silenced spaces are themes that underscore many of the subsequent generation of poets who continued in this work during the process of the return to democracy in Chile, Uruguay and Argentina in the mid-1980s and throughout the 1990s. In their summary of the tendencies in poetry in Chile at the end of the previous century, Rodríguez Saavedra and Chandía Fica argue that "Formarse una idea de la complejidad en sus variantes de la actual lírica chilena es dilucidar la motivación—casi genética en nuestra sociedad—que provoca el acto reproductor de una especie en extinción, cuyo nacimiento fue absolutamente ineluctable y marca sin duda el devenir del milenio que sigue" (2000, page 1 of 8, online). ("To envision in all of its variants the complexity of contemporary Chilean poetry is to elucidate its motivation—almost genetic in our society—that provokes the reproductive act of a species in extinction, whose birth was absolutely indelible and without doubt marked the future of the millennium which followed") (translation mine). One of the tendencies in the poetic language they note as a factor in many of the 104 poets included in their overview is the move from the use of the lyrical first person subject to a "textualized I" ("un yo textualizado) as in the epic poetry of Homer ("de un mundo épico") (Rodríguez Saavedra and Chandía Fica, 2000, 1).

Moreover, Nelson places the observations of Chilean poetry and art actions within the context of a critique of the tensions between a hegemonic world order that entrust the fate of the Pacific Southern Cone country to its economic successes, an amnesiac stability which plows forward without taking into consideration the effects of the previous decades' political and social costs. With that in mind as an overall context, Nelson indicates the relevance of considering the new poets' challenge to the "collective reticence regarding recent history and the consumerist orientation of city life under the hegemonic neoliberal model" (201). As per Nelson's view, Prado and Urriola "posit the political importance of poetic memory, of sketching tentative lines of affiliation with, or counterproposals to, symbolic gestures of the past" (201). In this regard, *Poesía es +* was created to be received spontaneously by passersby as an unexpected means of critical reflection on the role of poetry in social processes. An additional element was to invoke beauty over spaces marred by a horrible past: "Cuando agoniza la belleza emerge el horror.// Frente al horror: poesía" (When beauty lies dying, horror emerges. Confronted with horror: poetry)" (Urriola and Prado 2004, 77; cit. in Nelson 2007, 201). If it is not a gesture of escape, then, as Urriola and Prado have both confirmed, the intervention is a method of resistance; what, then, is the alternative proposed? The contrapuntal nature of this action illuminates a new ideological stance—moving forward from the previous avant-garde actions, without abandoning their lessons or achievements.

Vicente Huidobro's work comes to mind. *Altazor* (1931) is the main example from Chilean literary history that posits flight, or a descent from a celestial height, as a new perspective on reality. As posited by Huidobro's theory of *Creacionismo* (1914-1931), in the years affected by World War I, poets and artists were to replace the space created by devastion and loss, which had resulted in such tragedy up until then, with something new. Words were actual things that created new objective reality, albeit residing exclusively at first in the mind of its creator; and these words were to act in and upon the world, rather than describe it. According to Huidobro, this was the mission of all true poets. A sense of beginning anew, in a certain sense, went hand in hand with this perseptive, although the image-driven power of such a poetic vision was rooted in the Aymara oral poetry of Bolivia shared by a an indigenous person of the region with Huidobro. A returning to the roots of this creationist impulse will also be a quality evident in Vicuña's work, to which we will turn subsequently in this chapter. The return to the lost past in order to envision a new future, therefore, is present in *Poesía es +* and in the gestural and sound expressions that Urrioal and Prado engage in to perform the work.

Furthermore, some discussions of the *Poesía es +* have approached it from a mythological perspective. Benjamín Chávez has questioned whether "the parallelism between poetry and height" (Chávez 1) in the work can be linked "tangentially or referentially to Hanouan from India, Mercury, Daedelus or Icarus as remote references of events that we could classify as poetic, as moments of creation and invention" (1). Urriola responds this question in an interview with Chávez, explaining in what way the allusions to flight in *Poesía es +* are:

> gestures of escape in front of that which has been built. […] Our proposal to soar precisely […] the rarified airs of a modern-postmodern Latin American city consisted, rather, in more than an escape. It was a poetic intervention in the city of Santiago. […] we wanted to visualize a poetic constitution, once devastated by the esthetics of a mass market. Since these ancient flight vessels are used by market in the area of publicity to promote consumer

products…we wanted to fly there and read out loud with a megaphone for anyone to hear and see our vessel from the past, as poetry is also a vessel of the past. The modern human being never looks up to the sky. The modern human no longer believes in poetry. (cit. in Chávez 1)

The four events were conceived, according to Prado, to be "the intervention on spaces marked by the hidden history of Chile, in order to reconfigure the call to memory, in a country without memory" (Chávez 4). Notwithstanding the insistence on the classification of the art actions as "interventions," it is notable that these are realized using a soft version of flight, that is, that of hot air balloons, falling paper, and a small plane—by no means, turbo-charged as emblems of the twenty-first century and its scientific marvels. The slower approach is also a statement about returning to a more inward stance of contemplation of the natural surroundings, and of allowing that landscape to intervene in the creation of meaning.

Vicuña's Andean Sky in the City: Unmaking Dystopias

Chilean-American poet, artist and activist Vicuña puts in practice that questioning and poetry's capacity for agency in the awareness about premade socio-political structures, in turn proposing alternatives. At a scholarly conference held in October 2012, Vicuña was one of the keynote speakers and initiated her presentation by entering a low-lit room while streaming skeins of raw wool throughout the space. Singing softly, she walked between the dozens of rows and held the wool over the heads of audience members of the large university auditorium, inviting a few to hold portions of the wool. As she made her way methodically to the front of the room, leaving zigzagging streams of raw wool in her wake, we could also see at the front of the hall a large screen upon which were projected images highlighting prior exhibits of her works—these included black and white images of the same art action that took place at New York's harbour with Vicuña and other women participants, as well as interspersed words on a black screen, featuring her poetry. When she arrived at the podium, she delivered a poetic lecture, using a slow humming type of speech that approached singing, while retaining a whispering quality. In her lecture, Vicuña asked audience members to consider the nature of reality and poetry's ability to intuit its larger contours, as well as to place this re-enactment of her work, *Cloud-Net*, into resonance with her mention of previous urban interventions and public and private gallery installations based on this work since the late 1990s.

For Vicuña, the way to approach the world and its reality poetically is through weaving words and other physical objects together, as reclaimed discarded pieces merge into new configurations. The means by which they are transported from body to body, however, is their tactile and flowing nature. Metaphors of movement, of fluids within and between bodies of flesh or of the natural surrounding environment, blend with and inhabit larger metaphoric spaces of air, wind and sky. Poetry as a vessel through space is also, then, a key to meaning construction, as we saw in *Poesía es +*. Displacement is a theme that underscores all of Vicuña's installation art and poetry. Born in Santiago de Chile in 1948, she was exiled in 1977, four years after the military coup that removed Salvador Allende from power. She now makes her home in both New York and Chile. She writes in Spanish and English, sometimes in the same text, and often intersperses indigenous words and references in her poetic constructions as well. Vicuña has said that she aims to express how "the non-local joins with the local, poetry writes itself in non-time. It "transcends across time" and "is pure information" (2012). Clark explains that it "replaces interrelation with intra-relation, or it is inter- e intra-relation simultaneously" (2012). The pregnant or enlivened womb as metaphor in Vicuña's *Cloud-Net* represents the space that is non-spatially determined.

For example, in another work titled "A Menstrual Quipu: The Blood of the Glaciers Journal," feminine revolt and sacred spaces of protest are written in relation to blood connections and the cycles of blood flow in the female body. On the exhibition listing on her official website describing this street performance, Vicuña explains that, "I bring out the censored red fleece and place it in front of the government palace, pleading in silence to our President that she not sell our most precious heritage, the glaciers: "El ruego es el riego, el agua es el oro, Michelle, no vendas los glaciares." [The plee is the irrigation, water is gold, Michelle, don't sell the glaciers.] (2006). At this installation/movable street performance, the location speaks of the past and the recovery of memory as an awakening point to avoid further error; at the same time it also offers a remedial stance, one of blood flow that can instead contain life-giving properties. As stated on the description of the street event on Vicuña's homepage, the museum where the performance with the Menstrual Quipu took place is located under La Moneda [which also means The Coin or Currency], "the government palace which was bombarded during the military coup of 1973 and recently restored" (official website of the artist). Also explained in the web text is the definition of the quipu: "(or Khipu): Knot in Quechua, ancient Andean 'script' or 'writing with knotted cords, used for oral poetry, storytelling, accounting and maintenance of communal rights and responsibilities" (website).

As in *Cloud-Net*, space is an elemental part of its appearance, where something of the artist's creation comes from an apparent nothingness of the streetscape set by daily public use. Several images of the performance show Vicuña dressed in tan slacks and a brown jacket holding and moving the long red wool skein from the entrance of the government building to the edge of the sidewalk, and it is later held by other women in a calm stream of visual representation of historical memory and environmental activism. The metaphor of the large river of menstrual blood holds these messages, yet also proposes a dialogue with the female President. The November 9th entry for the exhibit posted by the poet reads as follows:

> Opening night. Michelle Bachelet doesn't show up. The Minister of Culture, Paulina Urrutia, comes instead. I give her a copy of the letter, telling her of my request to Michelle: 'don't sell the glaciers, water is gold.' She listens, and says, 'yes, Michelle will come to see the show.' 20,000 copies of the poem with a red thread begin to be distributed. Most Chileans don't know about El Niño del Plomo, or that he was found with a red thread. The red thread may be a symbol of union. The Incas conceived themselves, (the

> totality of their culture), as a quipu, seen from below, or from above, radiating a vision of the world from Cuzco into the four directions, all the way to the river Maule in the South of Chile. The work acquires a new name: 'The Blood of the Glaciers." (2006)

The frozen mummified remains of the Boy of Plomo, an Incan child, were found on Cerro el Plomo (Hill of Lead) in 1954; it is believed that he died in an act of human sacrifice by the Incas. The November 9 version of the exhibit is changed into what the artist deems a "weak version" of the quipu, as it had been censured on November 6 due to other artists' complaint that it offended them. Vicuña's entry for this day, titled "censorship" explains the rejection of her work by others, including her fellow exhibitors:

> Offended by the thick streams of wool, some artists in the show ask the curator to remove my work or diminish it in size 'because it is too big' (although it fits exactly the space assigned). Echoing their request, the curator asks me to undo the piece and create a thinned out version. Outraged by this request, I wish to remove my work from the show, but then I see: the violence against the threads is the violence against the glaciers. In Chile, the subject of the glaciers, and the struggle against the Pascua Lama project have been completely removed from the press. Nobody mentions it, and I don't see art about it… so I decide to stay and create a 'Versión débil', 'a Weak version,' a wounded quipu that tells the story of the censorship it endured. (Vicuña's official website, 2006)

As in the above description, *Cloud-Net* emerges within a larger scope of meaning, shape shifting in response to the environment of its reception. The perspective rendered in *Cloud-Net* of being in and of the sky is carried in the wool, which in this case is raw, not dyed red as in *A Mentstrual Quipu*. It also drifts as a cloud floats and shape-shifts across the horizon, forming a natural part of its cycle within larger patterns. Bringing it back down to earth, the hand-crafted aspect represented by the act of weaving the creamy wool skein and the sensation of the fibers as they flow through the fingers of the poet-weaver, is another level of the grand cycle implied as a metaphor for creating and sustaining the natural world. The porous membrane of the graphic design of the wool as it is strung above the heads of the receptors who behold the installation created by Vicuña seems to not only echo the sky but bring the presence of the wool grid into close proximity as a blanket; it envelops each viewer and marks a collective space all at once. Vicuña also traces the link between the light gesture of weaving and unweaving the wool in constant motion, as a metaphor for time.

An additional sensory layer is introduced with singing, as she hums whilst she weaves. The tactile, visual and sonic elements thereby feed the creative act and, by extension, its reception in the experiences of the visitors to the installation. The iconography inscribed in the types of book reproductions and filmed performances of Vicuña's installations, as with the other installations, internet interviews and photo captures of the urban poetic interventions by other Latin American poets, such as the collaborations between Chileans Nadia Prado and Malú Urriola (1998, 2002, 2003, 2004, 2012; see also Nelson 2007) show themselves to be, as Prado notes, "ephemeral, yes, volatile, perhaps, but a register continues to circulate in some space, ...that tell[s] us something about the moment in which they erupt or that others make erupt" (cit. en Chávez 2). The culturally produced objects in print, as books or in film, therefore, stand in as signifiers for memory, on the one hand, and of echoes of the body's presence, on the other. Vicuña's *Cloud-Net* mediates the way poetic signifiers can be rethought and remade in each site.

CLOUD-NET: MAPPING THE SPACES BETWEEN

Vicuña's poetic texts put into practice what Einstein explains in his precursors to quantum science and its metaphors of the space-time continuum as akin to a womb. Yet it exists as a wave-like all-encompassing space that causes effects in material reality. Vicuña believes that "there is nothing in quantum physics that has not been said in poetry" (AILCFH Conference, October 2012). Tying this in with what we have been describing of the cosmic plenum model of reality, the womb of creation as an unseen grid represents the spaces between material reality. That reality is mapped as energy that solidifies across wave-like space. Intersections at certain points creates appearances of materiality.

The proliferation and repetition of words, images and sounds in nonlinear threads in the digital and *world wide web* is what Vicuña translates in her poetry as this organic sense of extensions of our thoughts and sensations into her *Cloud-Net* installation. For Laura Hoptman, "The title is a metaphor, but it is also a neologism" (in Vicuña 1999, 12). It spatializes the connections in a woolen net that also transports the viewer to Andean heights, a bird's eye view of the geography of the Americas, as well as a sense of familiar comfort.

The poetic image of a cloud woven into a fragile semblance of a net, something that cannot exist, according to Vicuña (1999, 12), reflects what Kristeva writes in 'System' about the contradiction of the untheorizable *chora* "located at the centre of the semiotic entreprise; she writes that "[b]-eing, because of its explanatory metalinguistic force, an agent of social cohesion, semiotics contributes to the formation of the reassuring image which every society offers itself when it understands everything, down to and including the practices which voluntarily expend it." (from System 53; cited in Moi 162). Since the "*chora* is a rhythmic pulsion rather than a new language. It constitutes, in other words, the heterogeneous, disruptive dimension of language: as contradictions, meaninglessness, disruption, silences and absences in the symbolic language" (ibid). Since it cannot be closed in a static space, it can only draw a grid around the fullness of the empty space that surrounds physical space, becoming a pulsation or pressure on the linguistic system. Its negativity in relation to spatial determination nonetheless does not preclude it from affecting material reality. This precarious space, situated yet ephemeral, has associations with the internet and our personal-impersonal interactions, as well as with the *chora* as the sound space of being connected. There are also echoes of Kristeva's "not touchable" sense of self that is beyond the material and yet has a sense of its own being.

Vicuña considers her texts "poesía vital" [vital poetry, poetry that has life, or life-giving poetry] that is pure information, and which registers in the subject's body as its moves through its surroundings, and in non-local space, simultaneously. The title of the work came to her from a poem by Sri Aurobindo in *Savitri*, that she found while preparing her texts and working with the wool. The Savitri text reads: "We who are vessels of a deathless force / ...messengers of the incommunicable /...one day shall change the suffering earth / Delight shall sleep in the cloud-net of her hair / And in her body a music of griefless things shall weave" (cit. in Vicuña 1999, 28). These verses serve as epigraph for Vicuña's *Cloud-net*; the book contains a series of 40 photos of the three installations described above, juxtaposed with twenty of her poems.

Neither Prado nor Urriola nor Vicuña posit the subject in the work in a solely maternal function, although it is creative, as it moves toward the re-signifying process. Indeed, the non-determined gendered spaces of the poetic subjects move along the relationship to the body as secondary to the more immediate human sensations. This is beyond sexuality as attraction or desire as pleasure for its own sake, although the sexual impulse is not absent nor does it preclude its various expressions. Nowhere, though, do we see in the selected texts a reversion to subjugated gender roles. This freedom from the Lacanian symbolic and from the fetishization of the maternal body by feminisms as a counter to the paternal law, allows these poets to recover their neutrality, or a return to a different way to envision subjectivity as between the genders, as interaction, rather than as a biological stasis or singular starting point. At the same time, it refers to "'actual' subjects" (Magroni 96). While "Kristeva retains the maternal/feminine connotations of the *chora* (Magroni, 95)" this,

> does not mean, however, that she is not aware of the dangers involved. In *Des Chinoises* (also published in 1974 [as was *Revolution in Poetic Language*]) she cautions against letting 'Woman' be turned into the 'Truth of the temporal order...an unrepresentable form beyond true and false, and beyond present-past-future' (Moi 1986, 155). This is why in her introduction of the semiotic *chora* she emphasizes the need to remove it from 'the ontology and amorphousness where Plato confines it' and to 'restore this motility's gestural and vocal play...on the level of the socialized body'— which is precisely what this ontology leaves out . (95)

Magroni, therefore, notes this aspect of the *chora* as "subject to biology" (95) but to "a *socialized* body, in other words, a body that has crossed to the other side and has taken (is always ready to take) 'a chance with meaning' (1987, 235)" (Magroni 95). Thus, as Magroni concludes in her analysis of the "lost foundation" (2005) of the *chora,* in Kristeva's "discussion of the *chora,* it is the maternal body that is foregrounded, whose function cannot be reduced to that of a mere metaphor, 'a metaphor for transgression'" (Walker 1998, 125) or for a forgotten and forbidden *jouissance*. Rather than point to an enigmatic essence beyond it, it draws attention, instead, to the immanent material process of which it is a part, the 'Event In-between' (as we have called it) that reinscribes the speaking subject as the product of an alternative form of relatedness despite/in-difference" (Magroni, 96).

The role of the maternal body in this process is two-fold: metaphorical and situated. On the one-hand, it epitomizes the mechanistic aspect of the process that cannot be traced back to one or more particular female subjects, which would then serve as its source or as agents within it. On the other hand, as a *socialized* body, it opens up the process to the embodied experiences of 'actual' subjects, for the situation and situatedness of the maternal body are lived differently by different women" (96). Magroni sums up Kristeva's position in that:

> It is precisely this openness of the *chora* to a restructuring prompted by the (mechanistic or social) other that renders it, not essentially revolutionary, but what Protevi calls 'a permanent revolution,' which is how he invited us to think of democracy (2001, 192). In the context of this revolution the maternal body is neither an alias nor an alibi for the other but a socially experienced situation of alterity that compels us to rethink our relation to the other (*and* others). In reclaiming what has (culturally at least) formed part of female experience for both male and female subjects, Kristeva warns us against reading the event of the *chora* as essentially feminine. (Magroni 96)

When applying this dual aspect to *Cloud-Net*, the womb as wave-like grid stands over the specific site of the enunciating body that creates through singing, dancing and weaving.

Meredith Clark has identified the "maternal drives that generate linguistic production" in Vicuña's work such as in the textile-maternal bond projected onto the body (2012). In the first verses of the book, handwritten words appear as a thread across the page making reference in Spanish and English to the "mother of the clouds" and to a request uttered to "please let her through" (Vicuña 1999, 24–25). The *chora* is evident in these visual poems as "they disrupt the signifying order of the linguistic system" and return a "maternal dynamism" (Clark) that defines the poetic articulation. For Clark, the graphic text opens the poem to multiple interpretations and is a material conceptualization on the page.

For example, in her poem whose first verse is "hanging by a thread," the positioning of the first word [hanging] on a vertical axis leads into the second verse: "by a thread"; the white spaces and dispositions of the rest of the poem are laid out across the page in a zigzag design, released from the standard left-to-right graphic display of typed text. The next verse introduces the subject of the poem's main verse: "the web" which "says: www // we will weave // […] a weeping door / and stones at your feet" (30). This is also a play on the acronym for the World Wide Web[7] made up

---

[7] We could recall also that the *World Wide Web* (www.) was created at CERN in order for physicists to be able to share date quickly across the globe (Levinson, dir., *Particle Fever*, 2013).

of the three w's. Perhaps inherent here is a play on the word 'w/o/man'—a mirrored negation or addition to the etymology of "human" or "person" that derived interchangeably with the term "man". In this poem found in *Cloud-Net*, it is the "web" that "says: // we will weave" (1999, 30). Contrary to the Law or logos of the Father-God, the web appears sexless, a plural voice (30). It then describes space (height) and igniting of energy: "web up / web on" (30). To extend the feminine metaphor further, the association of cyclical life and unity of all creation can be applied here to Vicuña's use of weaving as a motif. As Micea Eliade summarizes, these aspects connect to the moon as symbolic of "harmonies, symmetries, analogies and participations which make up an endless 'fabric,' a 'net' of invisible threads, which 'binds' together at once humankind, rain, vegetation, fertility, health, animals, death, regeneration, after-life, and more" (180). Citing Eliade's work, Veronica Goodchild explains in her book *Songlines of the Soul* that "this binding quality helps us see why the moon in so many traditions is personified by a deity, or lunar animal, that 'weaves' a cosmic veil or net. In many of the images of the goddess she is wearing a garment with either spiral designs, crescent or labyrinthin motics, or net-like patterns. These rich associations reveal the moon as a beautiful sumbol for initiation into the subtle body and subtle words" (Goodchild 362–363). Although commonly associated with the feminine, the moon and its cycles of life and death, and with fecundity/fertility often have a masculine archetypal association, too: Osiris as moon, water and vegetation, in connection to his sister-bride Isis; the ancient Egyptian moon god Khons or Khensu who controls the waters of the Nile; the Babylonian god Sin who stands on his crescent moon boat; Shiva, "moon god of the mountains and carries the crescent moon in his hair (Goodchild 356). The unity of these archetypal aspects are what is prevalent in these images, although the moon is predominatly associated with the feminine symbols in nature, with tides, rains, and menstrual cycles.

Morever, the reference to height in Vicuña's verse "web up / web on" afterward flows downward in tears toward the "stones at your feet." This brings to mind the Western symbol attributed to the female sex, with its origins in the ancient Greek symbol for the goddess Venus, formed by a circle, representing spirituality, above a cross, representing matter. Alchemists subsequently used this symbol for the element of copper (masculinity, by contrast, was symbolized by iron). Copper is the oldest known metal, after gold and silver. According to a site dedicated to the exploration of its symbolism, "[t]-he earliest form of Venus was the Egyptian ankh, symbol of universal life; the egg-shaped womb of the goddess, the place where life is generated, surmounting the cross of the elements. This womb from which the sun emerges is represented by the copper cauldron of alchemy. It is interesting to note that the Christian religion removed this womb-egg from the ancient symbol of life, to be left only with the unbalanced cross of matter" (Borderlands 2011).

SINGING, WEAVING, SACRED TEXTING

The interchangeable feminine/masculine faces of the sacred appear in another poem of the collection, titled "the decipherment" (Vicuña, 1999, 52–53). In this 22 verse poem, which begins, "the masculine *ah* / in the head of the God C / / K'u, called 'the sacred'," is a reference to the Yucatec Mayan word for "divinity or sacred" and likely symbolized the Monkey god. However, the sacred is called "sexless" in subsequent verses--from the sixteenth to the end of the verbal text (52). On the opposite page of the words of the poem, Vicuña has placed an image taken from ancient indigenous texts of the Hunab K'u, also considered the "Sacred One," the "Supreme Being, the Unique Bearer of Movement and Measure" (Men 33) which the Maya and Aztec worshipped in Mesoamerica at the time of the arrival of the Spanish conquistadors. This symbol was shown in geometric form as a circle and the square in architecture. The Incan also depicted Hunab K'u geometrically, and believed that "all that is manifest, animate and inanimate, is merely a projection of energy, of God, and so they employed the concept of universal geometry in their traditional architecture, depicting the circle and square, thus sealing their conviction that God is energy, and energy is God" (Men 35). In Vicuña's poem (in English in the original), this reference links the architectural and the textual:

> K'u, called 'the sacred'
> and the syllabic sign *na*/house
> were read *ah k'u*
> 'of the sacred house'
> a knot
> in the *na*
>
> said *hu-n*(a)' (52)

The poem continues to explain that "the book / is the knot // the scribe / *ah k'u hun* / 'of the sacred book' " (52). The sacred, which is a knot belonging to this house: "knot book / sexless // the ah [not italicized in the original] / neither a he / nor a she // scribes / equal / in the knotting" (ibid). Kristeva's notion of the *chora*, developed from the earlier Platonic definition, and by-passing certain Lacanian essentialization of this theorized feminine, would be best read in conjunction with Butler's performativities, to liberate the *chora* from the female biology. Furthermore, if the reproductive function in Kristeva's theory of the *chora* is a metaphor for a type of articulation of signs that resides in both the male and female bodies, as part of the subjectivities of the psychological make-up of each person, this frees us from the roles prescribed to our biological sexes by the normative socio-political matrix in which most of our actions take place.

The definition of metaphor employed here is based on Paul Ricoeur's concept as established in his 1975 work "La Métaphore vive" (Paris: Seuil; first published in English translation in Toronto in 1977, we refer here to the 2004 English edition translated by Robert Czerny, based on the original manuscript by the author). I bring these together in this chapter to consider that, if science can use metaphorical examples to illustrate its conceptions, it thus must exist first in the imagination, as faith, as a story, as an image to be tested through experience and proven through mathematical reasoning. Ricoeur (1975), as well as Hawking and Mlodinow (2012), recur to Aristotle to illustrate the Occidental stages of the study of reasoning processes since the fourth century B.C.; the latter, however, discredit many of Aristotle's scientific assertions because they were not based on observation; see their chapter, "The Rule of Law," 2012, and specifically pages 22, 33–34 and the chapter "Choosing Our Universe," page 35.) Ricoeurian hermeneutic phenomenology places importance on observed experience and on the reception of the perception of the body for its compositional proof; yet, it does so textually, through discourse. Subsequent work by Ricoeur focused increasingly on sociological implications and on ethics in the political arenas (1981, 1986, 1995, 2000 and 2001). Therefore, the metaphor belongs within this ontological search for truth telling, not merely are representation of fantasy or of the imagination as dislodged from the phenomenology of being in the world and of social agency.

In other poems of the collection, in addition to indigenous words, Vicuña integrates both Spanish and English translations of these verses. Photographs of the three *Cloud-Net* installations (as the one on page 31 of the 1998 Buffalo exhibit) serve as counterpoint to the poems' visual display on the pages. This is a constant reminder that for Vicuña, "The poem is not speech, not in the earth, not on paper, but in the crossing and union of the three in the place that is not" (14). The impossibility of separating the speaking body from the earthly situatedness or from the textual expression imply a continuity of creation, being and recognizing self as part of a larger matrix.

REALITY-MAKING: WEAVING WITH QUARKS

The urban art interventions by Prado, Urriola and Vicuña seek to harness energies that would move each person out of the solitude and powerlessness of individual separation to give primacy to in-between spaces built by the textual fabric of inter-subjectivity, interactivity and thought patterns made material. However, these positions never confuse, erase or conflate the singular self into a collective homogeneity. Rather, a dynamic exchange grows exponentially in spaces previously given over to purposes other than pure utilitarianism or predetermined objectified exchange. They serve as a reserve to liberate from any totalizing effect. *Poesía es +* and *Cloud-Net* return to the oral proximity of the body, its voice, to highlight the ruptures or pulsations that interrupt the symbolic order as a defense in the face of trauma, loss, and danger. The voice in a living body now replaces the articulation of the pre-imposed law in print as solidified matter beyond malleability. This does not undo all law; merely law the as monolithic and stagnating. It returns to the organic space of meaning production in the waves of sound frequencies morphed into language and its many signs. Neither does the poet-performer-activist of this calibre forget the "intervention of print" (14), as Rosa Alcalá points out in her edition of Vicuña's a recent collection of her poetic performances, *Spit Temple* (2012). In it, for example, we find a poem titled, "*The Poetic Key. Santiago, 1963–64*," that speaks to the relationship of the oral and the written in her poetry:

> My first writing had the archaic flavor of Golden Age literature. I read like

> crazy, encyclopedias and comic books, novels and poetry, until I found two books that opened the door for me: the oral poetry of the Mbya Guarani, collected by León Cadogan, and surrealist poetry by women, translated by Aldo Pellegrini. Instinctively, I fused them. Hearing the way I read them I found "my" tone and "my" language. (50)

The corporeal aspect of her works, highlighted in the performances she offers in different locales, goes beyond just sounds and written signs; they literally thread memory into actions with found objects and an encountering experience with physical spatialization. As Sara Kellner affirms, each time the artist positions the woven sky art installation in a different urban space, she created "a new neologism" (cit. in Vicuña 1999, 12), a new way of addressing an experience of reality.

This dimension of *Cloud-Net* poses a counterpoint also to the world of the internet and the predominance of specular images found in media broadcasts and other popular forums. She thus gives prominence to touch and sensation in a way that not only speaks to memory. In an interview of Vicuña regarding this work, New York writer David Levi Strauss poses a question regarding how she situates herself in the "digital" world, when this "no longer has anything to do with our fingers, it means saying yes or no very rapidly. [...] Do you have that sense that textile, in its tactility, is more memorious than the word?" Vicuña responds that: "Perhaps, but I don't know because, you see, I am a mixed person, a person of two cultures. So I don't trust either—that is the reality. I use everything because I want to ask them all to remember. I write, I sing, I weave at the same time, because I'm at the moment of emergency, at the moment of danger, when you actually feel that all of this could go away. Life itself could go away. The web can disappear. So I work on that edge" (in Vicuña 1999, 20). The spaces of memory in Vicuña's word-bodies and her installations, as a way of "weaving against death" (1999, 53), preserve what she refers to as a "proposal to listen to the images... [to] the ancient inhabitants of the Amazon [who] spoke of the mist of the mountains" in order to remember" (53). Memory is harnessed by the sound of the voice and in the body as textual/historical marker.

In another poem published in this collection, *"The Heresies Collective, 1980,"* Vicuña refers again to the intertwining of performing poetry with political engagement (2012, 86). Prado asserts that "in poetry there is provocation, but I rather call it resistance, not as a non-reflective provocation, but as a resistance in the sense of guarding a poetic language that is being lost, resistance as opposition to the violent hegemony of money. This is a resistance that is opposed to the prevalence of the economic global machine of the first world. Without a doubt, we will not be able to stop the advancement of economic devastation of our countries, but we can still set up a word that infiltrates into the discourse of media, devoted to money and war" (cited in Chávez 3). For Prado, poetry recovers the spontaneous malleability of intimacy in which "language is capable of rethinking the prevailing codes and is capable of innovation" (2003, 2). As in Prado and Urriola's *Poesía es +*, this occurs at the level of representation both in creating the poems, together with the photographic texts, and in their reception, through reading and listening to their sounds in performance. These poetry acts counter the prevailing symbolic ordering of language to privilege experimentation. The potential gained for opening new ways of perceiving an alternative desired reality demonstrates how language, visual imagery and sound expressions can be channeled into new political awareness.

CHAPTER 3

Performative Reading and the Multimedia Novel

EMBODIED TEXTS AND MUSICAL READINGS

Usually music and literature as signifying systems are studied separately, as parallel forms; yet what interests me here is the way they influence each other. Developments in the novel since the 20th century in Latin Amerrica have provoked the questioning and overlaying of the musical and literary devices and discourses which writers found necessary to describe their reality in truer ways. By juxtaposing musical references and rhetorical parallels to musical effects in their writing, many were able to communicate various dimensions of the world they describe and to incite the participation of readers in new and provocative ways. Works by Cuban Alejo Carpentier (Cuba, 1904-1980) and Jose María Arguedas (Peru, 1911-1969) in the earlier part of the 20th century and as precursors of the *real maravilloso* aspects of the region often brought the musical and oral aspects of language and culture to bear upon the literary word, as well as historical revision to incorporate aspects of racial tensions in Cuban identity, in the first, and of *mestizaje* in the second. 'Boom' writers such as Gabriel García Márquez (Colombia/Mexico, 1927-2014) and Julio Cortázar (Brussels/Argentina/París 1914-1984) readily acknowledged the profound influence of orality and music on their narrative work. Manuel Puig's narrative work, such as his most internationally recognized novel *Kiss of the Spider* (1976) incorporates well-known boleros sung by the homosexual protagonist, Molina—an aficionado of Hollywood—to fellow prison inmate, Agustín Arregui, who shares his jail cell in a fictionalized Argentina during military dictatorship in the 1970s. The gendered consciousness of these themes related to postcoloniality and the revision of history can also be found in a novel by Ángeles Mastretta (Mexico, 1949-), *Arráncame la vida,* for instance, and in *Bailar con la vida* by Zoé Valdés (Cuba, 1959-); the latter invokes a more contemporary view but they share traits such as the appearance of sensuality and music in relation to questions of identity, exile and political turmoil.

In her second novel, *La ley del amor* (1995), the best-selling author of *Like Water for Chocolate* takes the reader through a tripartite construction of narrative text, music and comic strips woven into a complex web of signification. It retrieves a mythical/historical archive of Mexican colonial and postcolonial references via a sci-fi romp across seven centuries, from 1527 to 2180. The characters of *La ley del amor* are cross-gendered, hybrid constructions that challenge the reader to re-enact the storyline by dancing at specific moments. At one point, the reader can imagine the memories of the fictional characters alongside musically accompanied "regressions," while at other intersections of text and compact disc, the reader is asked to tune in to the recorded *danzones* and actually dance. Arias as well as the poems of the nahuas of the *Cantares mexicanos* also play a dominant role in the narrative plan.

Since its publication few novels have appeared in this multimedia format, with accompanying compact disc containing songs and sound effects, comic "clips" and musical meta-textual references. Recent examples, such as American author Joseph Coulson's *Of Song and Water* (2007), which integrate jazz improvisational techniques in literary language, come closer to Latin American novels by authors such as Julio Cortázar's *El perseguidor* (a novella, first published as a short story in 1959 as part of *Las armas secretas*) for instance, where a "musical" sense of reality superimposes itself on other perspectives.

In a different way, Ángeles Mastretta's *Arráncame la vida* (1985) was one of the first feminist perspectives on post-revolutionary Mexico and an example of the *bolerización* or "hibridación de la novela" (Mora, 2000). As per what Luis Rafael Sánchez termed earlier as "prosa bolerizada" (1988), the novel is 'set to music' so to speak by adopting lyrical forms and references to well-known boleros of tropical America. Yet as with most novels involving music, such as the bolero, the creation involves the same elements of the abstraction of music to memory or recreation as a concept, be it as a symbol of national identity or of a historical period.

Among these types of novels that use the bolero in their narratives we can mention those published by Dominican authors such as Pedro Vergés, *Sólo cenizas hallarás* (1980), Marcio Veloz Maggiolo with his *Ritos de Cabaret* (1991), and Enriquillo Sánchez with *Musiquito: Anales de un déspota y de un bolerista* (1993). These and other novels also reference at times the musical subgenres of bachata and merengue, including Vergés' 1980 novel and *La bachata del angel caído* (1999), as well as *El hombre del acordeón* (2003) by Veloz Maggiolo. For in-depth studies of these works see Julie Seller's *Bachata and Dominican Identity / La bachata y la identidad dominicana* and the research of Fernando Valerio Holguín (2008, 2002a, 2002b, 2000, 1999).

While *Arráncame la vida* is also an historical revision of the political in Mexico, similar in some ways to what we see in *La Ley de amor*, Mastretta's novel remains centered in the literary as its communicative vehicle. The title alludes to the name of the bolero by musician/composer Agustín Lara "El Flaco de Oro" (1897-1970). Music is filtered through reading of song lyrics and remembered tunes of well-known boleros and a famous performer of Lara's music, singer Toña "La Negra" Peregrino (1912-1982) who actually becomes a character in the novel. This blends cultural history and fiction even further. Nevertheless, as a textual construct, Mastretta's work rests on musical history as a repository of aural memory for the reader, who must in turn be knowledgeable in that area, to draw upon those allusions and fill in the gaps of the text that give it a full sense of its revisionary critique of Mexican society and the political aftermath of the 1910 revolution. Highlighted throughout the book are, as its title suggested, the themes of love, gender relations and social norms for women. Moreover, the technology of print production had yet, in 1985 when Mastretta's novel was published, not reached the ability to include recordings within its pages. Jodi Picoult's *Sing you Home* (US, 2011) comes with a compact disc as *La ley del amor* did, and accentuates the sonorous elements for its own narrative purposes. Another recent novel, *Too Far* (2010), by Los Angeles author and musician Rich Sapero is accompanied by a 12-track CD titled *Dawn Remembers*, performed with Maria Taylor. It is now available on Kindle, Google Play and the Book App for IOS (see www.toofar.com).

Yet even though *Sing you Home, Of Song and Water* and *Too Far* use music as a bridge to access childhood encounters with the conflicting balance between the real and the ideal in a back-grounding soundtrack function, Esquivel's *The Law of Love* reaches beyond the use of the musical cd incursions in the text. Her novel incites a different level of questioning about the performativity of shifting identity constructions. The possible (re)appropriations of identity serve to counter the effects of an increasingly neoliberal, globalized, post-Cold War world order. The novel subsumes counterhegemonic perspectives, while also recognizing their contradictions. It is simultaneously self-effacing and self-affirming, while positing collective action as plural and individually led. On another note, while more critical attention has been bestowed upon questioning gender identity associations in the novel, such as in Claire Louise Taylor's "Body-Swapping and Genre-Crossing" (2002), less attention has been paid to the sensory interplay of the reading of Esquivel's novel and its implications for literary culture's creative power to displace hegemonic, pre-established colonialist and postcolonial binaries. In this chapter, therefore, we will examine the performativity of reading: how the transformative capacity of participatory, embodied reading displaces previous notions of reality-making and how it attempts to guide readers to new experiences of inscribing alternative realities in their own bodily response to the text.

In her writing, such as in her multimedia novel *La ley del amor*, translated to English as *The Law of Love* in 1996, Esquivel incorporates a complex web of relationships between neighbours, friends, family, love and professional colleagues in a mythical representational space. She places the actions on a time line that spans from the 16th to the 23rd centuries, localized mainly in the unifying geographical location of what is today known as the capital city of Mexico, D.F. Some interplanetary voyages and flights into space intersperse the action when the action is placed in the 22nd century, however, these serve as plot devices, rooted mainly in a televised and hyper media-regulated world of our times, and its relation to police thrillers and investigative stories of crime, political intrigue and explosions. Readily recognizable visual-spatial icons of the Mexican geographical space also serve to transport readers to embodying the novel. The use of Aztec mythology, text, and the pyramid in particular as a central motif, point to a re-articulation of Mexico's historicities and mythologies and how they interact with current conceptions in Mexico. By extension these are generalized in the topic of love and the laws of the world as applied to seeking it.

THE TIME-TRAVELLING, TRANSHUMAN PROTAGONIST

Azucena, the astro-psychologist, protagonist, is the centre of these webs of relationships. Her love story initiates the novel's plot; she changes body three times during the course of the action, and also builds links between all the other characters. Her career as an astro-psychologist brings to mind another such protagonist, Silvia—an Argentine who lives in exile in Brazil—in Manuel Puig's *Cae la Noche Tropical*

(1988), who is also at odds with her situation in her search for love, and is caught between various political ways of being.

In *La ley del amor*, the time factor increases the scope and complexity of these considerations by amplifying the number of analogical connections between historical relationships in the clash of cultures during conquest and colonization, as well as nationalism and regionalisms, the fight over religious dominance of ideas and structures, and finally the fight between good and evil as reflections of the spiritual connection to the earth and to others which in the end dissolves duality and resolves these in unity through the power of forgiveness.

Narrative Structure and Music

The narrative voices in *La ley del amor* espouse an awareness of the sensory linked with thinking beyond daily frenetic tasks. There is a central organizing narrative voice in the third person that also permits first person accounts by supernatural beings: Anacreonte, Azucena's guardian angel, and Mammon, the demonic guardian of Isabel, her nemesis. These voices filter the thematic and philosophical debates of the novel, the struggle for consciousness that is also determining the choices of the characters. While these angelic beings are outside of time, they do possess human traits and are not what they should be according to traditional religious doctrine. For example, they have a need for love relationships; the guardian angel swears profusely; and the demonic being defends suffering as a necessary good that is meant to save humankind. That is, these supernatural beings focus on mortal life and its intricacies. Their speaking to us directly calls us into dialogue with them on another level than the actions we are recreating in the other chapters. This requires active and participatory interpretation of the narrative structure, above and beyond the integration of music and comic grids.

Being present through imagination in a novel spanning more than eight centuries can be a challenge, one that Esquivel addresses through the use of music and an accompanying CD-rom. It is virtually impossible to avoid becoming aware of our senses and of our responses to music when we are focused on its relation to a text in this way. The first track appears at the end of Chapter 4 and is a musical excerpt from a "Dueto de Amor" from Puccini's *Madame Butterfly*, in a 1995 recording performed by the Orchestra of Baja California. There are 11 musical tracks in total: six from Puccini's various works; four danzones interpreted by popular singer-songwriter, composer and actress Liliana Felipe—born in Argentina and who has resided in Mexico since 1976—with their kitschy-cool nod to the past the danzones, such as "Mala," "A Nadie" and "San Miguel Arcángel," are similar in tone to another track of a comedic dance number, "Burundanga," composed by Latin artist Oscar/Rafael Muñoz Bouffartique's (track 3), possessing strange playful lyrics and which was made popular by Celia Cruz. These musical pieces, all vocally strong in style and representing a wide range of historical periods, are interspersed at key moments of the plot across the sixteen chapters. The last track combines a fragment of Puccini's *Turandot* with fragments of the "Saludo Caracolas—Quetzalcoatl, 4 elements of the Canto Cardenche; Versos de Pastorela."

To illustrate, we can take the example of how Esquivel renders this by inserting in *La ley del amor* an aria by Puccini: "O Mio Babbino Caro" by Gianni Schicchi, is included as track 4 on the novel's CD (1996, 119-126). The musical recording is to be listened to by the reader during the first regression to a past life. This traumatic event depicts the 1985 earthquake in Mexico City in which two of the novel's characters are depicted: one is a baby in the regressed memory—in effect, the protagonist in the novel—and the other, is a murderous woman who kills her with a rock in the midst of the crumbling city—who in the present tense of novel is her archenemy, Isabel, in the year 2200 (1995b, 119-127). This episode also connects with a previous allusion in the text to the karmic cosmic cost of a colonial violence inflicted symbolically atop the Pyramid of Love in Tenotchitlan in the first chapter of the novel (1995b, 11-12):

> La casa, pues, quedó habitada por seres que no interactuaban unos con otros. Por seres incapacitados para verse, para escucharse, para amarse. Por seres que se rechazaban en la creencia de que pertenecían a culturas muy diferentes. Nunca supieron que la verdadera razón era una que nadie veía. Que el rechazo provenía del subsuelo, del choque de energías entre los restos de la Pirámide de Amor y la casa que le habían construido encima. Del / rechazo total entre las piedras que formaban la pirámide y las que formaban la casa. Del disgusto de la pirámide que no esperaba más que el momento adecuado para sacudirse de encima la pierdas ajenas y así recuperar el equilibrio. (Esquivel 11-12)

> (The house, thus, became inhabited by beings who did not interact with each other. By beings incapable of seeing, hearing and loving each other. By beings who rejected the belief that they belonged to very different cultures. They never knew that the true reason was one that no one saw. That the block came from underground, from the shock of energies between the remains of the Pyramid of Love and the house they had built upon it. From the complete rejection among the stones that made up the pyramid and those that made up the house. From the dissatisfaction of the pyramid that only awaited the appropriate moment to shake off the stones that were not its own and in that way recuperate equilibrium.)

This passage of the novel links the action to the 1985 Mexico City earthquake and a regression experienced by Rodrigo, as well as to an ecological and historical account of the war between cultures in Mexico.

Music and space cross over here in their historical reference points, and as symbolic representations. According to Veronica Goodchild,

> Pyramids, like Gothic cathedrals, were and are vast sonic temples. Again, we can remind ourselves that in both Eastern and Western religious traditions, sound, vibration, word or tone is present 'before' creation and is the force behind the visible manifest world. Think of 'OM,' or as some describe it the 'AUM,' also reflected in the Egyptian 'amun' and later the Christian 'amen.' The frequency of this sounding mantra arises from the solar plexus chakra

and is used to center and ground the praying individual or groups. Sound was so fundamental to an understanding of the universe that many of the teachers in the ancient mystery schools were musicians as well as initiated philosophers. Sound is thought to be involved in moving the massively huge stones vast distances to create the ancient stone circles and temples. [...] And in physics today the ancient music of the spheres returns in strong theory that now envisions invisible frequencies behind the constitution of so-called matter. (368)

The setting of the opening and closing scenes of the novel, as well as its historical romping through centuries around the need to replace its pinnacle or apex, serves as the grounding of the entire plot. The journey is undertaken thanks to the experiences ushered in through music. The progonist Azucena's role is to recapture a forgotten form of access to greater consciousness, a method through music that has since become outlawed by the 22nd century Mexican context of the fictional setting.

While continuing to instruct readers in the meaning of music for consciousness, within the fictional storyline, Esquivel also injects aspects of mythical and scientific knowledge about music as a vehicle for thinking and affecting notions of reality. As Goodchild also mentions, "since ancient times, music has been used in healing, from Aboriginal didjeridus, to Gregorian chant, to Indian classical raga music, and modern day ultrasound" (368). Azucena's aim throughout the novel is to use specific musical pieces to gain access to past life memories that will, as she puts it, heal the present trauma and unearth hidden aspects of life that will clarify the present. Many times in *La ley del amor* Azucena also mentions how music alters awareness. Indeed, the author herself, in the "Instructivo," which we will examine shortly, this insight into this aspect of altering states of conciousness and the relevance of using music as a guide to reading the novel (Esquivel 1996, 11).

By linking the text with music, the performative aspects of an aria or ancient Aztec ritual recitations of verse, or popular music dance rhythms, these all have an effect on the body even while we sit and read. The difference between silent reading and musicalized reading "ups-the-ante" for the reader by engaging the here and now as presence and relevance to complete the "as if" probability and close the distances between the text and the readers, and between readers. It also focuses the attention, and guides more closely the interpretative scope of the text. Students in my courses who have experimented with reading this novel, and have conducted surveys of the reading with its CD with readers of various age groups and cultural backgrounds, have expressed some shift and effect from playing the music during this textual experience. The mechanical impetus for straying from the book to an insertion of a CD into a sound player was considered an unwelcome intrusion on the act of reading for some respondents; however, when they did so, most admitted to feeling greater immersion in the world of the text in a way that was more heightened and visceral.

In this multiple, sensory space there is a marginal or peripheral revaluation where the subject can be de-centered, even fragmented, to another space. As Antonio Prieto states, "el o la performance"[*e*]-*s mutante gracias a su asombrosa capacidad de transformación en una hueste de significados escurridizos: parte del latín performare (realizar), pasa con el paso de los siglos a denotar desempeño, espectáculo, actuación, realización, ejecución musical o dancística, representación teatral, etc.*"(2). By likening it to the Aristotelian concept of theatre, Andrea Cabel suggests "it can be used as a metaphor of human action" (Portan9, 8 October 2011). In this sense it is similar to J. L. Austin's perspective in *How to Do Things with Words* in that every utterance that is not constative [capable of being judged as true or false] is performative, that is if it does not report something, it actually does something. In what sense, then, can we interpret Esquivel's novel as requiring a "performative reading" rather than merely functioning as representation?

To reply we must also take into account Judith Butler (following Austin), regarding her work in *Gender Trouble* (1990) and also in *Bodies that Matter*, in which she progressively works toward the definition of performativity. I posit that her notion of performativity reaches into the heart of this novel's theme of love and relationship. Dino Felluga describes this as taking "this formulation further by exploring the ways that linguistic constructions create our reality *in general* through the speech acts we participate in every day" ("Modules on Butler: II On performativity"). In this way, Butler's version is closer to our range of narratives and the structures of pitting music, text and image together in contrapuntal ways which offset any gaps of exclusion, thus producing a metaphor of human action that reaches beyond reporting about, and into performing or doing something about gender. As Felluga mentions, Butler's theory emphasizes that by "endlessly citing of the conventions and ideologies of the social world around us, we enact that reality; in the performative act of speaking, we 'incorporate' that reality by enacting it with our bodies, but that 'reality' nonetheless remains a social construction" (Felluga). According to Butler, "gender is an'act,' broadly construed, which constructs the social fiction of its own psychological interiority" (Butler, 1990, 279). In *La ley del amor* this fact is highlighted by the transference of sexes between lives and exchanging of roles, as we saw in the sample from the text.

Furthermore, for Butler, the symbolic musical sign represents the excluded aspects from what is normalized in the social constructions which "haunt signification as its abject borders or as that which is strictly foreclosed: the unlivable, the nonnarrativizable, the traumatic" (1993, 188). Puccini's arias in the novel appear when a character recalls the past to heal the present. When the musical track appears it is bereft of narration, although it is either aided by song lyrics or by comic grids that reenact a past occurrence in the lives of the characters that now is to be witnessed and felt by each reader. Not only does this serve to transgress gender boundaries, where not only are previously male characters "remembered" in these past life regressive memories as female, and vice versa, but it also plays up the place of the reader—whether male or female—to feel as if they were both and all the characters, even as babies who are in the early almost non-gendered stage. Where does that leave the question of cultural and political identity? Race and historical lineage are interchangeable and fluid, among the novel's fictitious, representative characters, as among the readers as they travel through time.

Here Butler's theory leaves less room to assist us so we can turn to other, more recent discussions on hybridity and trandifference to complete our reading of *La ley del amor*. Roland Hagenbüchle distinguishes this interplay as a defense of creolized identity that later developed into "the metaphoric notion of hybridity" championed by

Homi K. Bhabha (2002) and Salman Rushdie (1992). These postcolonial agendas war "against notions of racial and cultural purity and alleged superiority of white Western culture and its voracious appetite for global domination" (379); these theorists also recognize that "[o]ther civilizations have made similar attempts at hegemony but none has proved equally successful in the long run" (379). Hagenbüchle affirms the achievements of hybridity as an analytical tool, attributing to the "the function of a traveler's survival kit in crossing national, ethnic and religious borders" (380) and that it "has unquestionably raised academic critical discourse onto a higher and more nuanced level of self-reflection" (380). However, he also warns about the flaws in the notion of hybridity, namely that can potentially lack "critical perspective" (381) if not applied subtly taking into account the complex and sometimes contradictory aspects of identities. Instead, Hagenbüchle proposes the use of "difference" (382) based on ethical considerations. He sees as important the later works by Bhabha (2004, 2006) as crucial for their using Freud's concept of the "joke-work" (382). The use of the self-critical comedic perspective is a key element in marking a required distance to construct a "self ironic performance" with a "double-edged quality" (382). The humour integrated in the tone of the narrative voices (first and third person) reflects this stance.

Performative Reading

Let us begin with mapping the narrative strategy and establishing the chorus of voices that guides readers throughout the story. In the first edition of *La ley del amor* Esquivel include an "Instructivo" (Esquivel, 1995, 11-15) through which the first-person narrative voice explains how the book is to be read. This form of reading as game playing recalls works such as Julio Cortázar's 1963 novel *Hopscotch* [*Rayuela*] where readers could choose the order of chapters. Nevertheless, whereas Cortázar's format injected a free choice of chapter arrangement, thereby effecting alternating narrative outcomes, Esquivel's version of play centres on music and imagery that are more open-ended in their interpretations on one hand, while guiding the reader moreso in other ways.

In *La ley del amor* the reader's challenge in the 'Instruction Manual' describes choices that must be made to address the types of music to be incorporated into the reading experience—opera, popular music in *danzones* and other danceable rhythms; it also categorizes readers into three 'types' and indicates how each should proceed with the text. For example, for those who detest ópera, the narrator suggests: "¿Qué les puedo decir? Sé que de entrada se van a resisitr a escuchar el compact disc. Pero, para su consuelo, alternadamente con la ópera he incluido varios danzones que estoy segura van a ser de su agrado. Si esto no es suficiente para animarlos, por qué no se imaginan que están participando en un experimento nunca antes visto y que van a escuchar la música viendo las imágenes nada más para ver qué se siente o, si fueran ustedes creyentes, ¿por qué no ofrecen su sufrimiento a Dios o a favor de los niños desamparados?...pero óiganla, no sean cabrones, ¡no saben el trabajo que me dio convencer a mis editores de incluir el compact disc!" (13) And for the third category of reader who hates popular music she admonishes: "no sabe lo que se pierde, no hay nada más sensual que el roce de la piel, el intercambio de humores, el cruce de miradas, el trueque de mensajes eróticos bajo las ropas. ¡Anímese a contaminarse de sudores, olores, movimientos de cadera,. ...de vida!" (Esquivel 1995, 15). (You don't know what you're missing, there's nothing more sensual than stroking skin, the exchange of bodily fluids, the crossing of gazes, the back and forth of erotic messages under our clothes. Dare to contaminate yourself with sweat, smells, hip movements...with life!).

The opening guide also provides a caveat for a reader who cannot attune him/herself to the integration of the musical elements into the reading, and suggests they retire with a joint to enjoy it nonetheless in some way (15). The ironic tone of the writing underscores the metatext as commentary of itself as a new form of reading; what is ethical and postmodern at the same time, is a treatise beyond hybridity that celebrates a move into "transdifference." The freedom to choose specific musical pieces, however, remains that of the author. Furthermore, each the selected music is categorized and specified by Esquivel. Still, the associations drawn between the musical tracks and the narrative events are completetly in the purview of each reader, as is the decision to listen and when to integrate each track in the reading process.

It is interesting to note that the "Instructivo" was not included in subsequent editions of the book. Esquivel's overt reference to the innovative structure of the novel evident in her inclusion of the Instructive Guide in the book's first edition (1995) draws attention to the layout of the text, and is a metatextual awareness of the newness of her approach. By the subsequent editions (1996, 1997, 2000, 2004, 2009, 2015), multimedia components had by then become more commonplace to readers and thus perhaps the author felt no longer a need to instruct the use of the compact disc and graphic aspects of the novel to introduce her novel. As Debora Maldonado-DeOliveira argues, it could even more readily be published as an e-Book today (2011).

One of the interesting aspects of having the Instructivo available for our study is that it makes the reading focus on the gender of the author, as well as her intent. How do we know that she is a woman? The "Instructivo" is written in the first person voice of the author herself (1995, 11–15), and in the third paragraph she tells readers: "En esta novela la música forma parte importante de la trama porque yo ` de que la música, aparte de provocar estados alterados de conciencia, tiene el poder de sacudirnos el alma favoreciendo con ello la remembranza" (11) [emphasis in bold mine] (In this novel music is an important part of the plot because I am convinced that music, apart from provoking altered states of consciousness, has the power to shake our soul favouring our remembering.") In these pages, the author also admits that this book represents an innovation to the novelistic genre and thus she must instruct readers in how to read it together with the comic strips that are to be viewed along with specific musical tracks, and to put down the book to dance at certain points. To assist us in having a more vivid picture of the overall layout of the multimedia elements of the novel that combines all of these other genres, I provide below a structural map of the narrative. Each letter coded below corresponds to the following genres and elements inserted along with the narration, as indicated using the page numbers. The second edition is used for the map below given that this one indicated more clearly the chapter numbering, although it did not include the "Instructivo." The guide to each letter is as provided here:

a. Appearance of each regression: includes a series of illustrations as comics, without dialogue, that is to be viewed or "read" while listening to specified arias by Puccini[8].
b. Point of view of each regression
c. Historical period
d. Climax of the novel
e. Location of each epigraph and epitaph
f. Location of each popular song ("interludio") and its lyrics
g. Other musical and intertextual aspects

	1	2	3	4	5	6	7	8	9	10	11	12	13	14	15	16
A		R1 (40–48) t1						R2 (118–126) t4	R3 (140–148) t5				R4 (189–197) t7		R5 (220–228) t9	
B		Azucena (as infant)						Azucena (as infant)	Rodrigo (as female)				Azucena (as infant) (Citlali and Rodrigo appear)		Isabel (as male, Rodrigo's brother-in-law) (Rodrigo is female)	
C		1985						1985	1890				1527		1527 & 1890	
D															Azucena; Thematic	
E	(1;13) N Cm			(67) AC					(154) N Cm						(261–62) N R	
F	(14) Partial lyrics only		(61) T2 LF		(98) T3 OB					(165) T6 LF		(200) T8 LF		(233) T10 LF		
G																(251–259) T11 Finale

Figure 1: *La ley del amor* Structural Map
Source: *data adapted from Figueredo, Lecture Notes, AP/SP 4650 Literature and Music in Spanish America, York University, March 1, 2016*

There are various ways in which music is integrated into the narrative structure of this novel. (1) the use of the 11 tracks (on the accompaying CD-rom) that appear throughout the text, between chapters 3 and 16; (2) in various regressions, accompanied by comic strip illustrations and meant to be seen with one of the tracks indicated on the CD-rom: track 1 (T1), regression 1; tracks 3–4 (T3 and T4), regressions 2 and 3 respectively (T2 and T3); track 7 (T7), regression 5; track 9 (T9),

---

[8] It is important to note that one of the past-life regressions occurs not alongside an aria by Puccini contained in the companion compact disc. Rather, it is triggered necessarily by a cappella singing, when no listening device is available to the characters at a crucial part of the storyline. In this instance, Cuquita, who is Azucena's meddling neighbour, a stereotypically humourous type from a lower class in the telenovela paradigm of kitsch culure, who suggests that they regress a spoon, given its energetic memory of past events. While singing the danzón Liliana Felipe's "A su Merced" as part of the narrated events, Cuquita assists in advancing the plot and serves as a satire of the regression practice.

regression 6. (Please see chart "Figure 1" for details.); (3) the intertextual references/citations of the *Cantares mexicanos (Cm)* and the *Romance* by Nezahualcóyotl (N), and one of Ayoacuan Cuetzpaltzin (AC); (4) references to the mediatic function of music with regard to (i) narrative structure (in the "Instructivo" and on pages ...); (ii) made by characters throughout the novel; (iii) in what the supernatural beings describe; (iv) in relation to the plot development (D); (v) in function of the theme in *La ley del amor* of forgiveness and the various forms of love (collective—*agápe*; familial—storge; friendship—*philia*; and romantic—*éros*).

One question that springs to mind, among the many relating to the particular design of the musical aspects into the narrative frame, is why the citations the poems from the *Cantares mexicanos*, for example, of the nahua poets, (which are also mentioned by the narrative voice on the last page of the novel (251), are never cited in the middle of any chapter, but only at the beginning of certain chapters either as an epigraph, or at the end, como as an epitaph?

The subtext of the novel is its cultural allusions through the musical pieces, intertextual references to Nahua poetry and the incorporation of comic grids to the segments representing past life regressions. The interactive nature of the creation of the novel makes it a form of passive and active game playing. This is different from reading an e-book in that printed verbal text is still static. The text is not quite musical or visual either; the dependency of the text for creating the representational space and the thread of the action is also required. The desire to experiment is latent in the novel, yet it does not achieve all of its goals. The main failure lies in the dancing segments as these are seldom carried out by readers (according to a small case study conducted in a university course with research subjects within and outside the class setting). What it does do is communicate a multi-level perspective that calls the body to the site of creating the performance of the reading as each character and scene is recreated. The 'incarnations' are simultaneously, by extension, part of our selves as we travel through time and the imagination vicariously in the characters, sounds and images. The comics and the audio represent the emotional states of the characters and their roots in previous occurrences. The danzones are intermediate stages between chapters which are "like commercials," according to Debora Maldonado-DeOliveira (2011).

What Esquivel retains of the notion of hybridity, in Hagenbüchle's terms, is its "utopian core" (383). The goal of music, Esquivel writes, is to "shift our consciousness" (11) and to lead us, in the end, to a pervasive resolution of forgiveness for all, and unity at the heart of the pyramid of love which started the quest for order in the beginning (1996, 4). The original chaos unleashed by the Spanish conqueror's arrival and destruction of the sacred Aztec spaces in chapter 1, is restored 8 centuries later in chapter 16, after several reincarnations of the two central characters: Citlali, a Mayan princess and maternal figure, and Rodrigo, a Spanish warrior and colonizer, in 15th century Mexico cross time and swap bodies in various incarnations, and as Azucena and Rodrigo reunite as soulmates, until the end of the novel when they are all reunited, albeit in changed bodies which their souls jumped by trying to escape from authorities on their wild adventure. Thus, Esquivel's novel is not postmodern in the sense Lyotard gives the term if we take as our guide once again the position of Hagenbüchle who states that Lyotard's postmodernism prevented "the return of identity philosophy" (Hagenbüchle 383) and 'the moral point of view" as per Kohlberg (Hagenbüchle 386). While we agree with the postmodernists on the pitfalls of binary thinking—and dualisms are averted in *La ley del amor* in this postmodern way—it is also true that the novel goes beyond totalizing "difference" as a "heterogeneity" (383) that Lyotard would have.

As feminist Judith Butler posits in *The Psychic Life*, and postmarxists like Frederic Jameson would agree, we must "retrieve the subject as a responsible agent in political affairs (especially in gender politics)" and highlight "personal identity, moral dignity and autonomy, [...] freedom of choice, [...] responsibility and commitment" (383). What Hagenbüchle proposes is that "[a]s we may learn from Kant, Arendt and Kohlberg, the precondition of all dialogic exchange is the readiness to listen" (386); the focus on the sonorous and interactive is important here. What Hagenbüchle specifies is a "willingness to assume a [...] 'double perspective' [...], which is at bottom no other than a differential view signaling distinctions rather than likenesses" (386).

In this context, Kant speaks of an "enlarged mentality" and an enlarged self, and Hannah Arendt (echoing Cicero) of "representative thinking, to think from the perspective of others," as Seyla Benhabib mentions in this context-sensitive 'reversing of perspectives'" (cit. in Hagenbüchle 386). The body, thus, becomes the site of negotiating the 'double perspective' as the borderland upon which the difference is played out. The "borderline engagements" and "interstices" (Hagenbüchle 387) are the location "across which culture-specific views and social practices can be negotiated" (387); Bhabha's "Third space [...] notion of a nonsovereign subject" (Hagenbüchle 387-88) can create "a heightened awareness of the differences that separate us from others yet also link us to others through invisible ties which tend to form 'contrapuntal ensembles' (Said), inviting us to interact, contest, and negotiate" (388). This is achieved through the many aspects at play in the musical metaphors for time shifting and body transferences proposed by Esquivel.

In the fluid repeating spaces (Mexico and the other planets), it becomes more difficult to ascribe a static sense of belonging to a state, though it does not abandon a national identity altogether; seeking to avoid the corrosion of territorializing and frontier enforcing, Esquivel's novel espouses the sense of play in the musical, graphic arts as a way to connect subjectivities while also differentiating between ethical choices. As Butler and Spivak discuss in *Who Sings the Nation-State?*, our sense of place is a provisional, constructed space; as these are based on social and political agreements they can be refashioned to reflect our aspirations, instead of leading only to limiting our choices. In this sense, returning to our senses, as Esquivel suggests, is a two-fold perspective where we are the *Other* and the *Other* is and always has been "Us/me" at some point, or points, in time.

There is also more that could be discussed in relation to the position of "culture as resource," according to George Yúdice's 2003 study *The Expediency of Culture: Uses of Culture in the Global Era*. Here Esquivel pre-dates the post-September 9/11 context of crisis that Yúdice describes as the key to understanding the current post-national intermingling of the cultural, economic and political. The key, however, is what action is motivated or possible through culture to a resulting transnational and trans-institutional phenomenon (Yúdice 284).

In a similar vein, Rosa Alcalá discusses with Chilean artist, poet and activist Cecilia Vicuña on the poetics of performance that there is an increasingly renewed ability to consider the oral and visual elements of poetry, in particular, and in literature and our definitions of it. According to Vicuña who asks "Why now? Now is like the 60s, it's coming back. Now the students are tired of the oppression. They can't afford to study. So they feel drained. So the authority of the text cracks up, like the creaking up from the floor." Vicuña goes on to recall that in traditional cultural forms, "Poetry [was] not only 'literary' but had a larger definition." Oral culture was limitless." She argues that, while "academic definitions are limited," there are numbers of artistic projects that arise simultaneously in various cultures: "Community and communal culture are completely connected. [...] the collectives are coming back"... even though "They were looked down on for decades." (All of the previous comments are made by Vicuña; see interview of the artist by Rosa Alcalá).

The empowering, while destabilizing, voyage through various subjectivities echoes the fluidity between genres. The intermingling of oral, acoustic and verbal/literary forms is underscored not only by the presence and insertion of musical tracks and comic grids, alien to the traditional literary text, but also by the persistence of the presence of the Nahua poems throughout the novel. Not only do they appear at the crucial interstices of the text—in its introduction (1995b, 1), at the climactic moment, and at the close of the novel—but it its significant as the novel's implied "happy ending" is closely aligned with a vision associated with the past. It alludes to a coming full circle as the *Cantares mexicanos* also served as the opening text as well, positing a kind of thematic arch. At the beginning of the novel, we encounter the pre-Columbian citation of a poem by a 16th century transcription rendered by fray Bernardino Sahagún (1500?-1590) of the *Cantares mexicanos*. The last words of the novel are also granted to the same poet transcribed by Sahagún. The closing verses attributed to the Chichimeca sovereign, Nezahualcóyotl (1402-1472) of Texcoco, Mexico, stem from the *Manuscrito de los romances de los señores de la Nueva España*: "Percibo lo secreto, lo oculto: / ¡Oh vosotros señores! / Así somos, / somos mortales, / de cuatro en cuatro nosotros los hombres, / todos habremos de irnos, / todos habremos de morir en la Tierra ... / Como una pintura nos iremos borrando. / Como una flor, / nos iremos secando / aquí sobre la tierra. / Como vestidura de plumaje de ave zacuán, / de la preciosa ave de cuello de hule, / nos iremos acabando ..." (1995, 253)[9]. ("I sense the secret, the dark truth: / Oh my brothers! / Being mortal, being men, / four by four, all of us / have to pack ourselves up, have to die on the earth. / Like a painting we will fade. / Like a flower, / we'll dry up here in the dirt. / Like a cape made from the feathers of a zacuan, / from that rare rubbernecked bird, / we start to come apart the moment we leave the house."[10]) The particular nuances of the poetry of Nezahualcóyotl, "considered by his peers to be the greatest poet of ancient Mexico" (Curl 2003), were innovative for their time, and encapsulated a

---

[9] Nezahualcóyotl, "Romances de los señores de Nueva España," fol. 36 r., translated into Spanish by Miguel León-Portilla (1978).
[10] Nezahualcóyotl, translated into English by Forrest Gander (cit. in Zurita 2014 as epigraph, n.p.).

vision of the world that included peaceful political structure and cultural predominance. According to John Curl, "as the seventh ruler (*tlacatecuhtli*) of Texcoco, a large city on the north shore of Lake Texcoco, ten miles across the water from the capital of the Aztecs, Hungry Coyote [Nezahualcóyotl], promoted a renewal of Toltec learning based on the peaceful religion of Quetzalcoatl at the very moment when the Aztec cult of sacrifice was coming into ascendancy. All the Nahuatl-speaking city-states in the Valley of Mexico looked to Hungry Coyote's Texcoco as the cultural center of their world" (2003). Within than cosmovision, poetry was sung and its sacred dimension became, in Nezahualcóyotl's time, linked with individual expression of emotion and experience:

> Hungry Coyote lived at a moment when the anonymous singer, *cuicani*, of his people's tradition, who received verses in a song quest, began to speak of personal feelings and ideas and emerged a remembered poet. In form and content Hungry Coyote was an innovator: he perfected a style that numerous other poets copied. He was also part of a poetic movement, a generation of poets and singers who were moving beyond the earlier modes of Nahua poetry. (Curl 2003)

The "flower songs" (the more individualized poetic expressions) were performed with drums, while the older sacred hymns of anonymous authors were passed down collectively through memory by the elder generations.

By harking back to this blend of poetry and song, and its ritualistic and theological dimensions, Esquivel is linking the theme of her "law of love" to ancient belief systems rooted in a pre-Colombian Latin America. It is problematizing the notion as well of the lack of homogeneity of that past, as the Aztec rites of sacrifice, in ascendency during the reign of Nezahualcóyotl is unlike that purported by the latter's culturally dominant city. Indeed, inspired in the Toltec tradition, it also reaches back to a former way of being. Unity as a search for roots is accompanied by the blurring of generic distinctions between the written and the oral, as well as between the embodied practises of culture. Esquivel is positing a return to a society where the arts lay at the centre of all aspects of its functioning. In the time of Nezahualcóyotl:

> Singing and music were part of everyone's education. In the evening after school at the *telpochcalli*, the school for the common people, both girls and boys went to the *cuicacalli*, the house of song, which stood next to one of the temples. In the Toltec conception, a city did not really exist until it had established a place for the drums, that is, a house of song. ... Taught at these schools were primarily the sacred hymns and the dances that went with them. (Curl 2003)

Nevertheless it must be noted that the hierarchal structure of the Nahua culture separated the nobility from the common people. His aspects of social norms lays buried in the questions raised by Esquivel in her 1995 novel. Through recalling the past poetic voices of ancient Mexico—another poet, Ayocuan Cuetzpaltin[11], is also cited at the start of chapter 6 (76)—Esquivel signals a return to what I would like to term *choral thinking*, in which the individual expressions are not lost, but in which a common goal aligns politics and art, particularly vocal music. This paradigm appears to be a metaphor for Esquivel's theme of creating alternative futures through art and interactivity.

CONCLUSION: WRITING AT THE THRESHOLD AND CHORAL VISIONS

Esquivel's affront to a logos of narrativability finds its uniqueness in an open and potentialized play with the elements of storytelling—part sci-fi crime story cum comedy of errors for the post-new-age pseudo-scientific spirituality—that interweaves more serious reconsiderations of the nature of the text and our appropriation of meaning in dialogue through artistic expression in musical and pictorial forms. For Esquivel it seems less a matter of describing reality as of proposing alternative futures that we can envision first in creative expression. This links with what Veronica Goodchild refers to in her 2012 book, *Songlines of the Soul: Pathways to a New Vision for a New Century*, in what she argues is differentiated from fantasy or pure fictional creation. This is similar to Yúdice's critique of the shadow side of social creations; instead the "*mundus imaginalis*...[is] to be distinguished from purely imaginary or idealized ideas such as the notion of utopia" (17). In this definition, the "imaginal world is a 'really real' place where an interiority becomes the threshold to a new 'outside,' a spiritual landscape where beings have extension and dimension of a subtle or 'immaterial' kind. This is a world where space, being the outer aspect of an inner state, is created at will" (Goodchild 17). The empowerment of each individual is thus returned via the creative impulse.

For her presentation at the 9th Annual Writers' Conference & Literary Festival, Bilingual Conference for Writers & Readers in San Miguel de Allende, Mexico, titled "Creative Crossroads of the Americas," February 12 - 17, 2014, Esquivel lectured on "Writing the Future." In the promotional online material for the keynote address, she stated: "We can write a new story, a story that no one has written so far. That it is up to us alone. So far we have played the role of slaves, employees, hostages...but it's time we become creators and protagonists" (2014). Rather than describe reality to protest its flaws, Esquivel suggests we envision a new space, thereby initiating the design of an alterantive reality, one that can become physically and wholly integrated by enacting it. Esquivel's preoccupation with writing the future is intensified in more recent works such as her 2013 non-fiction publication *Escribiendo la nueva historia o cómo dejar de ser víctima en 12 sesiones*, which contains a series of exercises for creating personal scripts. As poet Jane Hischfieldstated stated in an interview published in *Psychology Today*: "Art is a field glass for concentrating the knowledge and music of connection. It allows us to feel more acutely and accurately and more

---

[11] A poet and wisdom keeper (from the Chalco region now in the Eastern part of Mexico City), whose name translates as "white eagle," he was and likely a leader of Tecamachalco between 1420 and 1441. The verses attributed to Ayocuan Cuetzpaltin appear on page 67 of the second edition of the novel.

tenderly what is already present. And then it expands that, expands us." (cited in Haupt). The use of writing for empowerment and change is a theme present also in *La ley del amor*, albeit with an emphasis on embodied creative expression through dance, visual reflection and musical allusion. The subsequent book takes interactivity further by inviting all readers to become writers of their own lives.

In a 2013 interview at the International Book Fair in Buenos Aires, Esquivel argued also that in *Escribiendo la nueva historia* she posited writing as a way to break with the past. Another well-known Mexican writer Elena Poniatowska echoed this idea in a subsequent lecture at Arizona State University when discussing the challenges to Chicano and Latino culutres and identities in the United States and to Latin American in general in the 21st century. Yet it is not posited by Esquivel as a singular event, but rather as an enacted form of engagement. Her use of the script technique highlights the oral and visual nature of this putting on a performance "as if" in order to bring it closer to being accepted as a collective reality. Esquivel describes the impetus for the book as relational: "Hemos vivido mucho tiempo gobernados por un sistema que nos hace creer que somos seres separados, que tu cuerpo termina en tu cuerpo y el mío aquí; que nada tenemos que ver uno con otro, con lo que ve y siente el otro. Eso no es cierto. Tenemos muchísimo en común y necesitamos romper esta idea de separación. Tenemos que dar ese salto, juntos" (cit. in Montaño Garfias 2013). ("We have lived a long time governed by a system that makes us believe that we have nothing to do with one another, that your body ends in your body and mine here; that we have nothing to do with one another, or with what the other sees and feels. That is not true. We have so much in common and we need to break the idea of separation. We need to make that jump, together" [translation mine]). The breaking with the past does not, however, eliminate all memory; its revision leave traces in the present. Memory is a starting point for the material process of writing. Through healing the experiences of the past, as the book's title suggested, the stance of victimhood is replaced by another option: that of performing our way into a solution.

In reading Esquivel's work, memory is assumed not as a repository for historical description and knowledge but as an access point to re/envision the future. *The Law of Love* suggests that living in the past is not a viable option if this entails only seeking justice for past wrongs committed against us. By structuring her novel in relation to canonical rules and rituals of ancient holy books, she reactivates the ethical questions raised in the text by testing various principles while also addressing the specific circumstances and the conditioning of the modern, technologically trained mind. Industrialization, globalization, pollution and technology present a new series of issues that require new thinking; these aspects are addressed in the novel through historical perspective, anacronisms, humour, drama, and sci-fi fantasy. The tongue-in-cheek tone of the novel makes it a more palatable mirror to hold up and instead view ourselves through the looking glass of literature. Music, in this case, as each of the selections have demonstrated, triggers specific allusions to cultural and historical contexts, in particular to that of a post-1492 (Latin) America, mythologized as Mexico. This mythical approach allows the reader to amplify the context beyond the geopolitical territory known as Mexico to envision a symbolic space connected across history and across time. Space travel, virtual reality television, teleporters, mind-reading devices and easy-to-swap biological avatars present in the novel reflect the author's views on the 21st century's dreams of the future. Esquivel therefore attempts to inform us, indeed urges us by prompting us to "perform" the text or enliven it with music. The purpose is to find the means to turn today's mysteries or crises into potential solutions or avenues towards enhanced realities. Nevertheless, the entanglement and contradictions of the institutionalized nature of the relationships of power structures remain inherent in the novel. The many levels of access and agency within these make for a complex and unpredictable course.

The last chapter of the novel includes a vast sonoric representation of the reestablishing of unity among all, once the apex of the Pyramid of Love is returned to its original location. The last paragraph before the fibal comic grid that accompanies track 11 (T11) of the CD refers to sound as the reigning perception hat ushers in the new harmonic reality:

El sonido de un caracol lejano se empezó a escuchar en cuanto pusieron la piedra de cuarzo rosa en su lugar. El aire se llenó de olores. De una mezcla de tortilla y pan recién cocinados. La ciudad de Tenochtitlan se reprodujo en holograma. Sobre ella, el México de la colonia. Y en un fenómeno único, se mezclaron las dos ciudades. Las voces de los poetas nahuas cantaron al unísono de los frailes españoles. Los ojos de todos los presents pudieron penetrar en los ojos de los demás sin ningún problema. No existía ninguna barrera. El otro era uno mismo. Por un momento, los corazones pudieron albergar el Amor Divino por igual. Se sintieron parte de todo. El amor les entró de golpe. Inundó cada espacio dentro del cuerpo. (Esquivel 1996, 243)

(The sound of a faraway seashell began to be heard as soon as they placed the rose quartz stone in its place. The air filled with aromas. A blend of tortilla and newly baked bread. The city of Tenochtitlan was reproduced as a hologram. Upon it, that of colonial Mexico. And in a unique phenomenon, both cities mixed together. The voices of the Nahua poets sung in unison with the Spanish friars. The eyes of everyone present were able to penetrate the eyes of everyone else without a problem. There were no barriers. The other was oneself. For a moment, all hearts could hold Divine Love equally. They felt one with everything. Love entered them suddenly. It flooded each space in their body.)

The eleventh track is accompanied by a series of 12 panels. These illustrations, six of which are full-page illustrations, mainly focus on the pyramid. This is the Pyramid of Love, as referred to in the novel, and in actual Mexico known as the Pyramid of the Moon in such sites as Teotihuacán, approximately 30 kilometres outside the D.F., that still remains quite intact, unlike that of Tenochtitlan, modern day Mexico City in which only recently have segments of the buried pyramids been excavated. Algonside images of the pyramid, which by the 8th panel is depicted near a Spanish colonial cathedral (such as the one that was built on top of the original pyramid in Tenochtitlan), there are citations of Spanish and Italian in the religious exaltations: "Huélguense a ver al Niño," "acabado de nacer," "Amor! ¡Amor!" (in the upper section of panels 2, 3 and 4 respectively); "o sole! Vita! Eternitá! / ¡Oh, Sol! ¡Vida! ¡Eternidad!" (panel 7); "Luce del Mondo é amore! / "¡Luz del mundo es el amor!"

(panel 8); "l'infinta nostra felicitá! / nuestra infinta felicidad!" (panel 9); "Ride e canta nel Sole / ¡Ríe y canta en el Sol" (panel 10); "Gloria a te! Gloria a te! / ¡Gloria a ti! ¡Gloria a ti!" (panel 11); "Gloria! / ¡Gloria!" (panel 12). (Esquivel 1996, 244-251). It is interesting to note that these captions are explicit in the first edition of the novel, but do not accompany the illustrations as of the second edition. The CD track for this "Finale" is a montage lasting almost two and a quarter minutes of the following compositions, as indicated on the song list: "Saludos Caracoles-Quezalcoatl, 4 elements / Canto Cardenche, Versos de Pastorela (frag.) / "Diecimila anni al nostro Imperatore!" (frag.) *Turandot* / Puccini" (Esquivel 1995 CD sleeve; 1996 264). The images on these pages depict the playing of the seashell by an indigenous character (panel 1), and subsequently the choirs of both Nahua and monk singers (panels 2, 3, 4 7 and 8) indicated in the preceding paragraph, as cited above.The placement of the apex of rose quartz appears with Citlali and Rodrigo in panels 5 and 6. The concluding panel is that of a Spanish cathedral superimposed upon the pyramic with the shining pinnacle stone at the lower central portion of the image (panel 12). The verses of Nezahualcóyotl, cited from the *Romances de los señores de la Nueva España,* close the novel.

There are two aspects, therefore, that have been examined here as crucial in considering the innovation of Esquivels' novel *La ley del amor / The Law of Love*: (1) the composition/production of the work of art, in this case a literary work with musical elements and references, and (2) its reception. In terms of its allusions to the abstractions of identity in musical references, this novel follows along a similar course to previous novels that refer to music as a marker of cultural identity, at least as a starting point. The presence of Mariachis, boleros, danzones and nahuatl poetry of the *Cantares mexicanos* in the novel point to a generalizing conception, at times mythical, in the configuration of the narrative space. However, Esquivel's novel goes further. By incorporating music by queer Argentinian singer/songwriter Liliana Felipe, it rearticulates and repositions the work of identity through these musical interludes at key moments in the narrative arch. A pianist, singer and composer born in Cordoba, Argentina, Felipe has resided in Mexico since 1978. Her first album, *El hábito* (The Habit) of popular music took its name from the theatre-bar in Coyoacán that she founded with her partner Jesusa Rodríguez. Most of the pieces by Felipe integratesd into the CD soundtrack of *La ley del amor* are Mexican-Argentine danzones. The danzón is a traditional Mexican rhythm, whose history is similar to the tango. Felipe later composed her own danzones. Of the total 11 tracks, Felipe's represent four out of five of the popular songs. The other is "Burundanga" by Cuban-American Oscar Muñoz Bouffartique (1904-), a composer and musician known for this peculiar song filled with jitanjáforas (or "sound poetry" as per Mariano Brull) and onomatopoeic elements. It was reorded in 1953 and made famous by Celiz Cruz and the Sonora Matancera. Furthermore, although the integrated musical pieces possess their unique historicities, the reception of the work by each reader differs in the way the genre and performative qualities are brought together by music and the musical interaction on the body of the readers/listeners, depending on the extent to which the "realized" execution of the musical portions (on CD rom) are incorporated into the final product as reading.

In the case of *La ley del amor*, both of the above aspects (music as *chronotope*, albeit a problematic one; and its ability to enliven reception) are present; these are guided by what the creative design of the novel has mapped out for the reader/listener (who each time chooses whether to activate the dancing and listening portions as prescribed by the narrative voice in the use of the compact disc). The way in which Esquivel transcends identity as based in one historical period or even as anchored in a planetary geo-positioning, calls into question the very identities presented as "Mexican," "Latin American" or "North American" on the one hand, as well as gender/sexual binaries, on the other, to post a transhistorical and transhuman, posthuman consideration of subjectivity. To what extent she achieves in harnessing the expression of all these possible identity structures and is able to represent them realistically is one aspects of the novel that has been seen as flawed (see Nehru 2004 and Taylor 2002, for example). Notwithstanting, Esquivel's multimedia novel also places in fluid questioning the place of reader in the creation of the text via the insertion of musical elements alongside the text.

Creation Sounds

CHAPTER 4

Sound Memory and Textual Tango

KEYS TO MEMORY

In Mario Benedetti's 1992 novel *La borra del café*, the protagonist named Claudio narrates about his life in flashback, autofictional format. The novel's twenty-ninth chapter, titled "El surco del deseo" (Benedetti 1992, 109–111), tells us how Claudio met one of his love interests, Mariana, while dancing tango in a social club in Montevideo:

> Es virtualmente imposibile que, después de varios tangos, dos cuerpos no empiecen a conocerse. En esa sabiduría, en ese desarrollo de contacto se diferencia el tango de otros pasos de baile que diferencia el tango de otros pasos de baile que mantienen a los bailarines alejados de sí o solo se les permiten roces fugaces que no hacen historia. El abrazo del tango es sobre todo comunicación (Benedetti 109)
>
> (It's virtually impossible that, after various tangos, two bodies don't get to know each other. In that wisdom, in that development of contact tango is different from other dance steps that keep dancers far from each other or only allows them fleeting contact that don't make history. The embrace of tango is above all communication.)[12]

Recalling this meeting with Mariana when he was twenty-one years of age, the narrator discusses his doubts about love and with whom to establish a closer relationship. The beginning of the chapter alludes to beginning "a stable relationship" (109) with Mariana, juxtaposed to athe mention of a Brazilian lover, Rita from Bahía, with whom Claudio had been maintaining a long distance relationship. In the context of developing his understanding of the nuances and complexities of the male-female relationship, Claudio muses on the way that the dance of the tango is a metaphor not only for sexuality, but also for his identity and art.

The overarching theme in the novel, and particularly in this chapter, is that of loss and absence remaining after the sexual/intimate encounter. The title of the novel, as well as that of the chapter, references this nostalgic tone. The music of the tango in the dance in the specific setting at the *Club Social Comercial* (109) reveals the "afinidad" (ibid) between he and Mariana, and considers it "algo infrecuente entre los jóvenes" (infrequent among young people) (ibid) for it belongs to a generation before them. Nevertheless, their affinity for the dance becomes a mutual understanding that

---

[12] All Spainsh to English translations from Benedetti's novel in this chapter are mine.

transcends verbal language. The metaphoric force of the understanding between them described as an "exploración mutual" [a mutual exploration] (109), is a signifier of the language of the body that unifies these two characters.

The function of the tango as signifier becomes, in Claudio's words, a "proyecto verosímil" (110), that will likely lead to an erotic encounter. A series of textual references to dancing tango acocompanies the development of the relationship with Mariana. Her presence and connection to the tango as deeper strata of communing is contrasted with the other women mentioned in the chapter, such as the housekeeper Juliska, a lover named Natalia with whom Claudio claims to have been "initiated" (109), and a strange fascintation with Rita. Although there is no specific model of the tango dancing specified in the chapter, there do appear various allusions to particular lyrics, songtitles as in for example "El choclo" and "Rodríguez Peña" (109). The tangos referenced in the flow of the text begin to alter the synactic narrative structure as the chapter progresses (particularly at the end of the third-to-last paragragh, which represents its dramatic climax). Indeed, at this point (111) the narrator confesses that he and Mariana "teníamos miedo de las palabras" (feared words) (ibid) because these could bring complaints, misunderstandings and mistrust.

As we examine each of the elements pertaining to tango in the chapter of Benedetti's *La borra del café* titled "El surco del deseo" that bridge various dimensions that it embodies for the main male character, Claudio, and his views on amorous relationships, subsequently, in the second part of the chapter we will focus on how a setting to music of the main elements and key phrases or whole syntactical structures from the novel is rendered in a new song by Uruguayan musician Winstron Mombrú.

Tango, History, Identity

There is a cultural subtext inherent in the mention of tango here whose historical grounding represents the relationship of time, memory and sexual awakening for the protagonist. But of which epoch? The specific allusions to certain titles of tangos and of a culture milieu associated with early forms of tango inform the references to this musical subgenre of the River Plate región in Benedetti's novel. According to Azzi, "The tango…is one of the defining factors in Argentine culture" (39). In Uruguay also, "It combines dance, music, poetry, song, gesture, and normative as well as philosophical ethics" (27).

"Gotán" is a word from *lunfardo* that means "tango." Winston Mombrú, a Uruguayan tango composer and singer, chose this as the title his 2005 compact disc compilation that contains a musical setting of some of the aspects, including complete phrases or sentences, found in Benedetti's chapter. Appearing as the ninth track of the CD, bearing the same name as the original chapter, "El surco del deseo" becomes a poem by Mombrú fashioned from words excerpted from Bendetti's narrative text. The accompanying CD liner notes indicate that the track is based on a *story* by the well-known Uruguayan author: "(Sobre un *relato* de Mario Benedetti) Texto y música: W. Mombrú. Interpretación: W. Mombrú (voz). F. Pérez (guitarra)" [emphasis mine] (Mombrú 2005). It is interesting to note this transfer from the page to a disc audio format. The compact disc, as a technological tool, was the favoured and up to date form of digital optical data storage when the novel and the music disc appeared. It would not be until after 2010 that alternative forms of recording data and music in particular would replace the compact disc and make it somewhat obsolete[13].

In addition to the track based on "El surco del deseo," the twelve-song complilation by Mombrú features musical settings of the poems of Juan Gelman (Buenos Aires, Argentina, 1930-2014), his interpretations of other famous tangos such as "Anclao en París" and "Mi Buenos Aires Querido," including one by Luis Aplosta and Edmundo Rivero titled "Poema número cero," and several original compositions. The cover of the CD by Mombrú cites both Benedetti and Gelmán: "El abrazo del Tango es sobre todo comunicación" Mario Benedetti" and "El Tango es una manera de converser" Juan Gelman" (Mombrú 2005). Two of the twentieth century best-known poets and writers associated with social justice themes and political protest, exile and ideology in the River Plate.

Benedetti (Paso de los Toros, Uruguay, 1920-2009) is one of the poets who sustained most collaborative work with musicians in his day, including producing peformances with fellow compatriot and classical/folkloric/New Song singer-songwriter Daniel Viglietti. His collaborations also extended across the Atlantic with Joan Manuel Serrat. Benedetti lived many years in Spain after his exile from Uruguay in the 1970s during the military dictatorship. He worked for decades with fellow Uruguayan Daniel Viglietti, especially with the various editions of the poetico-musical performances of *A dos voces* and *Desalambrado*. Perhaps one of his most extensive and broad partnerships were with Argentine musician, pianist and director of orchestra Alberto Favero (1944-). Their combined work on poetry and music began in 1972 with the setting of Benedetti's *Canciones de la oficina* [Office Songs] (1972), *Versos para cantar* [Verses for singing] (1972), *Canciones de amor y desamor* [Songs of Love and Unlove] (1974) and continued into the 1980s and 1990s with *Canciones del desexilio* [Songs for the end of an exile] (1983) and *Canciones nobles y sentimentales* [Nobel and Sentimental Songs] (1992). His poetry collection *Letras de emergencia* (1969-1973) and *Versos para cantar* are dedicated to two musicians: Nacha Guevara and Alberto Favero. With the exception of one poem ("Las ocho viudas" [The eight widows), all the poems in poemas *Versos para cantar* have been incorporated into the repertoire of one or more of the following popular singers/musicians: Nacha Guevara, Daniel Viglietti, Los Olimareños, Numa Moraes, Gianfranco Pagliaro, Soledad Bravo, Carlos Fasano, Dianne Denoir y Washington Carrasco. Benedetti is of the same generation of writers as Julio Cortázar (Brussels/Argentina), Carlos Fuentes (Mexico) and José Donoso (Chile) and shared with them the search of literary expression of ethical themes and political conscience. Many of these collaborations have been studied, especially in light of how the musical aspects affect literary culture and vice versa (for example see Midieri 1997, and Figueredo 1999, 2001/2002, 2003, 2005).

---

[13] The recordings of this compact disc have since been made available in digital file format online by Daniel Baccino at the following URL: https://sites.google.com/site/personaldebacci/musica/guitarra/winston-mombru.

Juan Gelman was also exiled from his home country, forced to leave Argentina in 1976. He subsequently resided in Europe, the United States and Mexico; he became a naturalized citizen of the latter, where he remained until his death. Like Benedetti, his political activism permeated his writings. His son and daughter-in-law were among the over 30,000 *desaparecidos* who were kidnapped and who disappeared during the reign of the military *junta* in Argentina. Never abanonding the search for his relatives, he finally was able to discover the buried remains of his son in 1990 and a year later to find his granddaughter Macarena who had been adopted by a pro-government family after the murder of her mother by police forces.

Both revered authors and respected for their defense of human rights, Benedetti and Gelman have been richly acknowledged as key figures in Latin American letters. They are also two poets who are often cited for their connection to popular music, either by having written lyrics for music, for reciting poetry with musicians, or for having their poems set to music. Benedetti, as well, is considered an indispensible reference point in the evolution of the Latin American novel from the 1970s until present day.

LA BORRA DEL CAFÉ [COFFEE GROUNDS]

La borra del café (Coffee Grounds) is one of Benedetti's most autobiographical works of fiction. Among his completed *oeuvre*, which include over 50 books and many literary prizes, this novel of the early 1990s is considered by some to be a collection of short stories arranged around a central character named Claudio whose life seems to follow a trajectory similar to that of his author. Throughout the forty-eight stories, or chapters, depending on how one wishes to view the book, we see Claudio grow up the age of five in a neighbourhood in Montevideo and the subsequent death of his mother. The book presents each of the stages of Claudio's life until adulthood. His career as an illustrator and painter for a commercial agency, his search for marriage with Mariana, and the trauma of the atomic bomb at Nagasaki all feature as part of his journey. In this way, he becomes a witness to many of the twentieth century historical processes seen from Uruguay.

Existential questions are placed alongside personal recollections of a space that recreates the Uruguay during the years just prior to the Second World War and into its aftermath. The novel/short story/fragmentary collection of anecdotes, thus, becomes a meditation on time, memory and personal reckoning with the past and present. One of the novel's epigraphs comes from a poem by Cortázar titled "El interrogador" (The Interrogator): "¿Adónde van las tinieblas, la borra del café, los almanaques de otro tiempo?" (Where do the shadows go, the coffee grounds, the almanacs of another time?) [my trandlation] (*Salvo el crepúsculo*, 1984) (*Save Twilight*, 2016). What is left from the years of remembering the lived experiences is highlighted in the book by Benedetti in his choice of epigraph, and is expressed in "El surco del deseo" metaphorically and symbolically in the tango as a vehivle of telluric connection to the Southern Cone, the River Plate region in particular. And as often occurs in Benedetti's texts, such as in the poem "Te quiero," of his most musicalized poetic texts by a myriad of musicians and interpreters, love and political conscience march side by side.

"El surco del deseo": Desire's Groove

Therefore, to examine the role of tango in this chapter is to see these themes of love and activism intertwined at the core, yet expressed in a fragmented literary discourse. How are they reflected in the discourse of the text?

"Surco" in Spanish can be translated into English as a groove (in terms of musical allusion it unveils new connotations in this sense), given that represents the grooves or spaces made in a record in which sound is recorded made by the needle as it glides through the spaces. It can also indicate a trace left by one thing on another, as well as a deep wrinkle or line on the face. "Surco" as a noun invokes a more natural paradigm of meaning: (in the earth) a furrow or the track of a wheel in the ground, (in water) wake or track, or (in space/air). As a verb, "surcar," can mean o plow through, or to cleave (in water), or fly through space/air (Oxford Spanish Dictionary 2009). By linking this verb to the act of desire ("El surco del deseo") in the title of this piece, Benedetti's text implies a grappling with what remains after the loving/erotic encounter. There is also a link to the book's title in *La borra del café* (Coffee Grounds) as another way to reflect on what remains in memory after livedvexperiences. As a metaphor of the mnemonic function, a connection to music is also inherent here.

It Takes Two…

The amorous relationship is at the heart of this 29th chapter in Benedetti's *La borra del café*. And yet its message includes cultural and social nuances that dance along with underlying currents of a specific Latin American political setting, within the coming of age story narrated. As the protagonist, Claudio, describes his life throughout the various vignettes that portray the Montevidean cityscapes and Uruguayan landscapes, it seems a crucial moment for his becoming an adult to reckon with this question of choosing a lifemate. Chapter 29, "El surco del deseo," marks a turning point in his identity construction, one that connects with his career in the arts, as a painter, and as a Uruguayan man. It is not until he meets Mariana that he finds this non-verbal communication enveloped in dance so important as a resolution to posible conflicts within the male-female dynamic.

These key elements of the tango as an expression of love is what Winston Mombrú will also pick up for his musical rendition of the Benedetti's anecdote. Of the three pages of prose that compose Benedetti's chapter, Mombrú selects key phrases, and at times entire sentences, to craft his poem-song:

> El baile de aquella noche
> Mariana…
> tanto acercó nuestros cuerpos
> que después del quinto tango
> se sabían de memoria.
> (Mombrú 2005)

(The dance that night

> Mariana...
> brought our bodies so close
> that after the fifth tango
> they knew each other by heart.)

Maintaining the first-person narrative voice, Mombrú's sung version of the chapter increases the dynamic energy of the song by addressing Mariana directly. The dialogue format, thus, enhances the duality inherent in Benedetti's theme of Chapter 29, even though in the original text there is no direct dialogue between these characters. In contrast, Claudio used indirect quotation about what they discussed, or rather, how little they spoke: "¡Hablábamos tan poco! Creo que teníamos miedo de que la palabra, al invadir nuestro espacio, nos trajera querellas, fracturas, desconfianzas. ¡Y el silencio era tan sabroso, era tan rico el tacto!" (Benedetti, 1992, 111) (We spoke so little! I think we were afraid that the word would invade our space, bringing complaints, taking a toll, bringing in distrust. And silence was so savory, touch was so rich!).

When words did come they were not of Mariana in dialogue with Claudio, but rather they were "otras y lejanas palabras" (other and faraway words) (ibid). They arrive in an envelope with postage of Bahia, Brazil; sent by another woman, Rita, who inquires about the progress of his art career, she represents a now past liason which he wishes to reléase. In her missive she writes: "Te felicito por la exposición. Me gustó tu aporte a mis agujas de las 3 y 10. [...] Besos y besos de mi boca débil en tu boca fuerte, todos de tu *Rita*" (ibid). (Congratulations on the exhibition. I liked your take on my use of the hands of the clock marking the time at 3:10. [...] Kisses and kisses from my weak mouth to your strong mouth, all from your *Rita*.) Although these words end the chapter, the preceding indirect discourse from Claudio implies that he no longer feels the same connection to Rita, now that Mariana is in the picture. This is signalled by his introduction of her cited letter with the use of the verb "irrumpieron" (111) (burst) when referring to the appearance of her written communication. No mention of Rita appears in the song by Mombrú, whose rendition focuses on the main topic of the tangos shared by Mariana and Claudio.

In the chapter following "El surco del deseo" the narration begins with Mariana; this 30th chapter is titled "Mujer del más acá" and within it Claudio debates her presence, against that of Rita's "más allá" (113). After taking a few days to consider his feelings, it is the spatial presence of Mariana and the trasnformation of their connection from the tango into something more profoundly sentimental that convinces him of his choice:

> De modo que cuando volví a ella, y le narré asimismo cuánto había pesado Rita en mis vacilaciones (hasta entonces nunca se la había mencionado) y le dije que me quedaba definitivamente con ella, el hecho de que eligiéramos, ella a mí, yo a ella, cada uno a solas y en libertad, significó un pacto espontáneo, sin papeles ni testigos, y cuando por fin nos abrazamos, por primera vez más acá y más allá del tango que nos había juntado, sabíamos que esto iba a ser perdurable, es decir todo lo perdurable que admite lo transitorio. (Benedetti 1992, 113)

(So then I saw her again, and I told also her how much Rita had weighed on my decisión (until then I had never mentioned her to Mariana) and I told her that I was staying with her for good, the fact that we chose each other, she chose me, and I her, each one along and freely, meant that there was a spontaneous pact, without documents or witnesses, and when we finally embraced, for the first time here and beyond the tango that had brough us together, we knew that this was going to be lasting, that is as lasting as the transitory can be.)

This dialectic between the meeting with the tango at the Social Club, and the week or so that it took to solidify their commitment, is foreshadowed in the initial paragraph of Chapter 29. This loosley chronological movement between the two chapters that allows for slight changes within them makes time malleable, as it can only be as viewed from the present as a memory. The reader is keenly aware of this flashback technique in Benedetti's novel as a means for an older Claudio, taking stock of the pivotal moments in his evolution. As the narrative voice confesses at the start of Chapter 30:

Habíamos hecho y deshecho el amor con una nueva, transformadora avidez, que no era sólo física; lo habíamos hecho con una dimensión del sentimiento que era distinta a la convocada por la conjura y la fascinación del tango. Era como si hubiéramos alcanzado otra región del goce, menos vibrante quizá pero más duradera. De pronto me sentí candorosamente hombre. No como antónimo de la mujer sino como sinónimo de ser humano. (Benedetti 1992, 112)

(We had made and unmade love with a new, transforming voraciousness, that was not only physical; we had made in with a dimensión of emotion that was distinct from that convocated by the spell and fascination of the tango. It was as if we can reach another leve of pleasure, less vibrant perhaps but more long-lasting. Suddenly I felt candidly a man. Not like the antonym of a woman but as synonymous with human being.)

Therefore, it becomes clear that this change is his outlook is described piecemeal over the course of both chapters, through narrative allusions to the tango as a before and after rite of passage to manhood, indeed, of a prologue to enlightened maturity.

Let us take a step back into Chapter 29 to examine the transformation to which Claudio refers. Subsequent to his meeting Mariana at the Club Banco Comercial, he narrates that days later, the sexual encounter makes real what had already been forershadowed by the the tango. This appears in the fifth paragraph of the chapter following the allusions to the cafishos of the 1900s and the popular tangos already mentioned. Here we see the sexual relations also as a dance of two bodies: "Así, los sucesivos tangos de aquella noche, que no fue mágica sino muy terrestre, permitieron que mi cuerpo y el de Mariana se conocieran y desearan, se complementara y necesitaran. Cuando, tres días después, nos despojamos de todo ropaje y nos vimos tal cual éramos, el desnudo textual nos trajo pocas novedades. Desde el quinto tango nos sabíamos de memoria" (110) (In that way, the successive tangos of that night, that wasn't magical but very terrestrial, let my body and Mariana's know and desire each other, complement and need one another. When, three days later, we shed all clothing and saw each as we were, the naked textuality did not bring any novelty.) Although he mentions that he will aim to paint a portrait of a couple dancing tango to capture the feeling of desire (111), the overall design seems more important that any visual cues of detail, colour or portraiture.

Curiously the visual aspects, so significant it would seem to a fine artist such as Claudio, takes second place to the overall image that is rather more impressionist and tactile, based in movement and sensation that is more akin to dance. The love-making is considered part of an "archive of the imagination" and a "memory of the body" separate from a detailed visual registry:

> Algún detalle nuevo (un lunar, siete pecas, el color de los vellos fundamentales) era por lo menos que subsidiario y no modificaba la imagen primera, la esencial, la que la disponibilidad sensitiva de cada cuerpo había transmitido a los archivos de la imaginación. La memoria del cuerpo no cae nunca en minucias. (110)

> (A certain new detail (a mole, seven freckles, the color of the fundamental hairs) was subsidiary at least and didn't change the first image, the essential one, the one that the sensitive disposition of each bodt had transmitted to the archives of imagination. The body's memory does not succum to minor details).

While glossing further over details of the setting and of Claudio's thoughts, Mombrú's song highlights above all else the central figure of the dance of two bodies, as evident in the first stanza cited above. The second stanza is taken from the following section of Benedetti's story, found in the latter part of the fifth paragragh, the longest in the chapter:

> El pecho que toca pechos, la cintura que siente cintura, el sexo que roza sexo, toda esa sabrosa red de contactos, aunque se verifique a través de sedas, casimires, algodones, hilos o telas más bastas, aprenden rápida y definitivamente la geografía del otro territorio, que llegará, o no, a ser amado, pero que por lo pronto es fervorosamente deseado. (110)

In Mombrú's "El surco del deseo" these images jumping ahead to the description of the embrace:

> El pecho que toca pechos
> el sexo que roza sexo
> aprenden la geografía
> del otro territorio. (2005)

> (The chest that touches breasts
> the sex that grazes sex
> learns the geography

of another territory.)

Condensing the encounter to its fundamental elements, in the song the sexual act moves from the two bodies reflecting each other in skin to understanding each other as a journey of discovering landscape.

At this point, Mombrú's text brings in what becomes the chorus of the song, as it is repeated twice in the recording:

> Es...
> el germen del amor
> en el surco del deseo
> bailemos otra vez. (2005)
>
> (It's...
> the seed of love
> in the furrow of desire
> let's dance again.)

After this summary, Mombrú musical interpretation chooses to cite the coital scene: "Tres días después / desnudos..." / tu lunar y siete pecas / no cambiaron lo esencial. // Recorriendo nuestros cuerpos / palmo a palmo confirmamos / el archivo imaginario / que nos dejara el tango." (2005) (Three days later / nude / your more and seven freckles / didn't change what was essential. // Exploring our bodies / inch by inch we confirmed / the imaginary archive / left in us by the tango.") The rearrangement of the original elements, some word for word extractions from Benedetti's text, and others (such as "Bailemos otra vez," and "lo esencial" as paraphrasing), serves to enhance the focus on the tango as the central motif for the amorous relationship. As in Benedetti, the tango's symbolic function for the erotic is not in the sense of pornographic visual detail, but rather as a vehicle for understanding the slow grasping of knowing another soul and its desirous movements.

The final chorus of the song repeats the chorus yet substitutes the present tense verbe "es" (is) with its preterite form "fue" (was), and replaces "bailemos otra vez" (let's dance again) with "amarnos otra vez" (loving each other again). The use of the elipsis in noteworthy after these verbs, as well as in two other verses, after "Mariana..." in the second, and after "desnudos" after the fifteenth. The usage of ellipitcal punctuation creates not only a type of suspension of words into feeling, but also imply that there is additional narrative beneath the musical version, thereby alluding to the textual inpiration for the piece.

What in Benedetti's original narrative had been stated as "es virtualmente imposible que, después de varios tangos, dos cuerpos no empiecen a conocerse" (110) (It's virtually impossible that, after several tangos, two bodies do not get to know each other.), in Mombrú it is summarized as: "what the tango left in us." The epigraph on the cover of Mombrú's compact disc recording takes another citation from Benedetti's story that echoes the original as we listen to his tango-poem: "El abrazo del tango es sobre todo comunicación" (109). It is reiterated in the inner sleeve of the collection of 12 tracks that includes the extended version of the quote (ibid) with which I began this chapter. However, Mombrú adds an elipsis at its end when he adds it to inner sleeve of his CD. The music of the tango is, therefore, insinuated as a type of communication beyond verbal language and supercedes the visual and verbal details. It imposes itself in a space between bodies, as an movement that creates a particular affective state.

Textual Tango

Syntactical and grammatical and other anti-conventional transgressions in Benedetti's literary discourse evident in "El surco del deseo" move the reader into a new space of meaning construction. Necesitated by the body's awareness of the references to tango culture and to the sexual act, the dance serves as a link to historical and socio-cultural memory as the narrator recreates his life story.

The deconstruction of the sentences in the last paragraphs of this anecdote reflects the succumbing to the reality of the body over that of verbal language. "Después de todo, / el germen del amor tendrá major pronóstico si se lo siembra en el surco del deseo. ¿Dónde habré leído esto? A lo mejor es mío. Lo anoto para el tema de un cuadro (sin relojes): El surco del deseo. Tal vez suene demasiado literario. Pero no. Debe mostrar a una pareja que baila tango. Sólo eso. El surco del deseo. Nada más. Que el público imagine" (Benedetti, 1992, 110–111) After all, the seed of love will have a better forecast if it is sown in the furrow of desire. Where have I read this? Maybe it's mine. I'll note it down for the theme of a painting (without clocks): The Furrow of Desire. Perhaps it sounds too literary. But no. It has to show a couple dancing tango. Just that. The furrow of desire. Nothing more. Let the public imagine.)

Music takes over in determining meaning, while grammatical and syntactical constructions are laid waste in the surplus of symbolism mediated by the dance and its sensuality. The geography of the body, or as Benedetti terms it the desired "geografía de otro territorio" (110) (geography of another territory), traces through the dance a series of implications for Claudio's recognition of his Uruguayanness, more so actually his River-Plate-ness, as vehiculized through the association with the tangos of a bygone era. The nostalgia superimposed on the past of his cultural references enlarges the field of meaning creation to assert a longing to belong, to connect and to insert himself in the cycle of history. This desire is expressed intimately through his connection with Mariana, whose presence a little over halfway through the collected chapters will be pivotal for his future.

By situating the tango of the 1900s in this way, both Benedetti and Mombrú reach back to a historical reference of the musical subgenre of the River Plate, that of the *Guardia Vieja* (1820-1920). This one, as compared to the more stylized and orchestrated subsequent generations of the tango (including post-Piazzola), harken back also to a wider cultural map of the musical references, including the origins of the tango in the *milonga* form, of gaucho heritage, as well as in the *habanera* and its African roots. (For a concise overview of the characteristics of the Old Guard tango, see Mesa and Balderrabano, as well as Ayestarán 1967; for further descriptions of the history of the musical subgenres of the *milonga* and the *habanera*, in particular with reference to literature, see Figueredo 2005).

Therefore, the mention of "cafishos" and to the two popular tangos already listed above, indicate a sexual and taboo aspect of the tango, making it even more poignant. Its anachronistic mention in the relationship of Claudio and Mariana, who were too young to still be keen on this type of tango dancing, brings them closer together. The nostalgia of the past, a somewhat Uruguayan national trait, is further traced in these two characters as a unique trait they share, as the text points out in the first quote we saw in my chapter's opening. As Claudio explains, it was the tango that set him off on the course that was to be significant for his love life: "Ya había cumplido mis veintiún años cuando empecé una relación con una muchacha estupenda. No sabría decir si éramos novios, 'o algo así,' como calificaba Juliska a las que, según ella, eran uniones irregulares" (Benedetti, 1992, 109) (I had turned twenty-one when I started a relationship with a great girl. I wouldn't know to say whether we were boyfriend and girlfriend, or 'something like that,' as Juliska used to say about those that were, according to her, irregular relationships).

The presence of Juliska brings to mind further information of the historical context of the chapter, also a part of Benedett's life in Montevideo, of the 1930s. At that time, Slavic women such as Juliska emigrated to Uruguay following crises in the Balkan countries after World War I. In terms of the relation of this character to the tango, as Eugenio Alemany describes in his annotated online version of Benedetti's novel: "esa avalancha de mujeres pobres nutrió también la prostitución de las ciudades portuarias. Así queda constatado en el término jergal del lunfardo, *cafisho*, que proviene de un término inglés adaptado por los proxenetas que controlaban este negocio" (36) (this avalanche of poor women nourished as well the prostitution in the port cities. This is validated in the lunfardo slang term *cafisho*, steming from a term in English that was adapted by those men who controlled the underground business). As Alemany suggests, "cafisho" was an Italian transformation of the English word "stockfish" used by the procurers to refer secretly to the "cargo" of women immigrants who arrived on ships from impoverished Europe; it was later adopted into lunfardo (as *cafisho, caffiolo* or *cafferata*) to mean "gigolo, pimp or freeloader" (68). "Lunfardo" is a popular jargon of about 5000 words associated with the lower classes that originated from an Italian dialect (of Lombardy) in the 19th and early 20th centuries in Montevideo and Buenos Aires. It is a criolle form that blends Spanish with Italian created by immigrants from Europe. The use of argot later expanded to the rest of Argentina and Uruguay and is closely tied to tango culture.

The insistence on historical memory ties in with Claudio's recollections. His lifetime parallels that of Mario Benedetti, born in 1920, and *La borra del café* makes references to Claudio's parents and various family moves to different neighbourhoods in Montevideo (from the first chapter titled "Mudanzas" or Moves, 10) in ways that echo Benedetti's life story. In the novel these collected memories work in tandem with Claudio's coming of age, as witnessed in the scenes of his relationships with women (Natalia and Rita, por example, mentioned in the chapter before "El surco del deseo" titled "Las tres y diez" (108). Therefore, time is as much a protagonist in *La borra del café*, as are love, desire and a sense of belonging.

The reference to the time stamp of "3:10" for instance is repeated in the 29th chapter, when mentioning the inclusion of his oil paintings in an art exhibit of young Uruguayan artists. His erotic depiction of dancing couples, women and clocks make up his style. According to the narrative voice, the public, who bought some of these works by Claudio, were most interested in the paintings that displayed the time as "las 3 y 10" or ten minutes past three o'clock. (108). The repeated mention of this time frame in the book indicates a pattern of understanding his trajectory in love's initiations. It is also an allegory of time's intersection with lived experience, in this case, of love, longing and loss. When set to music in Mombrú's musical interpretation, this time stamp disappears, along with the mention to Rita. Its focus rests on the tango and its force for recreating the scene in which love began for Claudio in his relatiomnship with Mariana.

The musical setting of Mombrú's piece reflects the intimacy of its theme. A quiet and dual arrangement features his voice and acoustic guitar (lasting 2 minutes, 17 seconds). Played in the disctictive tango rhythm of four beats per bar, it adopts the distinguishing feature of the subgenre, its syncopation, with increasing off-beats that favour emphases or accents that brings to life the passionate movement of the music as a dance as well as a heartfelt experience. The nostalgic tone of the piece embodies the space of memory, distancing the experience from the present, while preserving the poignancy of the affective stance it intends to recreate.

Nevertheless, the final lyrics of the song compound the nostalgia with a sense of repetition in the present. It changes the final verse to "amarnos otra vez," that is, "to love each other again" that underscores the cycles of love in Claudio's awareness. As in Benedetti's novel, which ends with a chapter titled "La borra del café," memory is a spiral that cycles back into previous experiences. Several mentions of the tango in the final chapter imply the dangers of sexual attraction hidden in the dance.

As Alemany explains, the symbolism of "la borra" of the novel's title is actually a reference to Rita, rather than Mariana. It had been prophesied earlier in the novel by a character named Perico, who was said to know how to "read" the coffee grounds in this esoteric practice of divination based on a ritual of making coffee and subsequently examining the remains in the bottom of a cup. Claudio recounts in chapter 21 that Perico had foretold a future for him that invoved a woman and a tree. In Claudio's mind, he related this is his meeting with Rita: "asumí mansamente el augurio, ya que a mi vez interpreté que, en todo caso, se trataría de Rita y de la higuera" (2012, 49) (I meekly accepted the prediction, since in my turn I interpreted that, in any case, it dealt with Rita and the fig tree). In the commonly accepted interpretations of the symbology of coffee ground readings, according to Alemany, a tree indicated that a project long in the planning would be realized (50). The parallel project that persists throughout the book in relation to Rita is unresolved until the end.

In the final scene of the novel, during which time the protagonist is on a plane travelling to a seminar that he will give in Quito, his mind summarizes all he has lived throughout the various chapters. Then, falling asleep, he dreams of seeing Rita again. In what appears to him at first to be reality, Rita approaches as a flight attendant and places her hand on his and kisses him provocatively. Previously in the novel it is clarified that Rita works as a flight attendant. Despite having spoken with Mariana prior to boarding the plane, and both agreeing to a life together, this dream aboard the plan of seeing Rita again elicits a sexual response from Claudio, much to his chagrin. The vertiginous flow of memories circle and encompass many references to the preceding 47 chapters, becoming a type of distillation of evemts. In the struggle between his letting go of Rita from his conciounsness, and the comfort represented by Mariana, the final battle is one rooted in the body:

> Por suerte del otro lado estaba el cuerpo desnudo de Mariana, y él logró apoyar sus brazos en aquellas cadera espléndidas, prójimas, tibias, y también logró acercar sus ojos a aquel ombligo único, de tango y de fruición, de trabajo y holganza, de juego y desafío, de consuelo y amor, y miró por él como quien espía por el ojo de una cerradura. Y por aquel carnal maravilloso orificio pude al fin ver el mundo, las calles y las praderas del mundo, un mundo con Nagasaki pero sin Rita, ya era algo. Y cuando el ojo de la cerradura volvió a ser ombligo de Mariana, apoyó su frente contra él y apenas murmuró: 'Mariana y punto.' (Alemany 2012, 103)

> (Luckily on the other side was Mariana's nude body, and he managed to lean his arms on those splendid hips, so close and warm, and also to bring his eyes to that unique navel, of tango and fruition, of work and leisure, of play and challenge, of comfort and love, and his looked through it as someone who observes through a key hole. And throught that marvelous carnal orifice I finally could see the world, the streets and the prairies of the world, a world with Nagasaki but without Rita, and that was something. And when the key hole of the lock turned back into Mariana's navel, he rested his brow against it and just whispered: 'Mariana, period.'

The final paragraph of the novel closes with the following conclusion by Claudio: "de ahora en adelante, nadie iba a hallar vestigios de Rita en la borra del café" (cit. in Alemany 103) (from now on, no one would find any traces of Rita in the coffee grounds). Therefore, the seed planted by love in Chapter 29 has, in the end result, rooted itself in a River Plate reality configured in the presence of Mariana and what she represents.

In conclusion, the tango in Benedetti's novel *La borra del café* encapsulates tension, and contradictions, even as it represents communication beyond words. Not only is it the vehicle of passion and sexual tensions of a relationship, it also pinpoints the dangers of such liasons, and the possible traps inherent in divorcing the sexual from the grounded connection of love. Mariana and Claudio's affinity for the tango that becomes their prologue to love, also harbours secrets (such as the relationship with Rita that Claudio initially hides and from which he must work to extricate himself, even until the end of the book. Whereas Mombrú adopts a more contemplative and peaceful stance in his musical rendition of the book's 29th chapter, Benedetti's text thrives in its constant tensions that force Claudio to finally make a choice. By using the tango culture of the Guardia Vieja in Chapter 29, Benedetti's text expands the personal references of this classic love triangle, to one in which historical intersections and questions of spatial belonging, resonate alongside nuances of existential questioning and values.

Creation Sounds

CHAPTER 5

E-Poetry: Videopoetry, Text, Aurality and Music

MOBILIZING THE BODY AS RELATIONAL RESISTANCE

In the online and on site works of contemporary Latin American poets, as in the case of three women writers we'll look at here, discrete elements of sound, gesture, visual and historical framing intersect with the poetic word to produce overflows of meaning across various geo-political spaces. By rethinking the staticity of the body in each reading/viewing experience, poems by these women writers reflect shifting notions of self across time and space, including ambiguous gendered positions of the poetic subject. The interpolation of the body is a function of the *performance* of the poetry (poetry as an oral act) and a function of the *representation* of the (real, natural, creaturely) body (as opposed to the ideal body, mechanistic-linguistic projection of the mind) within the poems themselves. By examining how these poets represent their countries in specific international events captured online, we see the attempt to salvage excessive ruptures of the relational self across time and space. Furthermore, we can observe how these poets' communicative strategies refrain from abandoning the body's situationality and historicity while their texts' performative aspects seek expression in shared spaces of plural performativity and alliance. Their poems in video, live performance and online privilige the expanded spaces of sound and movement, presence and gesture to lead the poetic thrust of their messages.

Melisa Machado (Uruguay), Lía Colombino (Paraguay) and Rocío Cerón (Mexico): Synchronicities

The three poets that I have selected for this paper—Uruguayan Melisa Machado, Paraguayan Lía Colombino, and Mexican Rocío Cerón—mobilize the body in projected works, redefining postcolonial memory and the location of the subject vis-à-vis the body—its sounds, its sensations as emblems of affect and of disengagement with surrounding cacophonies. While also negotiating the dissolution of the fixed unitary subject, as Marta Segarra has noted as the postmodern conception, poems such as these take into account the hypertextual and networked expressions of literature as a constantly relocating voice of the subject across shifting landscapes and historical vantage points.

As this pertains to three Latin American subjects, it is also important to note the difference in their conceptions of postmodernity, such as that described by Beverley, Aronna and Oviedo: "The engagement with postmodernism in Latin America does not take place around the theme of the end of modernity that is so prominent in its Anglo-European manifestations; it concerns, rather, the complexity of Latin America's own 'uneven modernity' and the new developments of its hybrid (pre- and post-) modern cultures" (12). Indeed, the historical pressing point becomes a new node of inversion for reinvigorating the enunciated expression. Nevertheless, in the post-postmodern iterations, the varying levels of subjectivation are not only unveiled as fragments—of the present and of memory—, of the self and its extensions to others, but as multiple points of access that can be recuperated via the body as decoding agent.

The drive for realization as a search for expression makes itself manifest through the body, despite its abstract considerations of deterritorialization and political paradigms. Poetry art actions and installations (onsite and online) invite moves in to freedom, connection, community and the rarified type of expression that merges the sayable with the unsayable. A process in constant movement, anchored in the body, plural connectivity shapes viewpoints and creates, or undoes, alliances in Pan-American environments. Seen in this way, Judith Butler and Athena Athanasiou's suggestion that we "think about the relational self, understood as plurality" (2014, 123), is an attempt to define this process via the term *dispossession*, as posited in the title of their 2014 dialogical work. Their inquiry brings to the fore the question of how to address the performative in the political in light of contemporary poetry online and its companion installations and the performed word at specific sites. According to their perspective, this serves:

> to confirm the importance of alliances and cohabitation across established categorizations of identity and difference, beyond the very polarity of identity/difference. The heterogeneity of precarious bodies, actions, frameworks, and affective states invites and requires continuous political work of engagement, translation, and alliance, work that veers away from essentialized understandings of identity and representation, and, of course, that effectively opposes nationalist discourses and practices. (123)

This view can also be considered in concert with the temporal aspects of hegemonic pressures to be faced by subjects, coinciding in some ways to what Heriberto Yépez has described in *The Empire of Neomemory* (2013).

With the threat of abstract concepts, and in particular to the imposed notions of imperial time and totalizing identities, there is a need for understanding the present via "biosymbols," to which I will return later and which we will see illustrated in the works of these three women poets. As Butler affirms, performative poetries such as these form "alliances [that] today are confronted with the challenge to engage in an intersectional political reconceptualization of class, race, gender, sexuality, and ability" (2014, 154). The double play and potential threat is evident in the term selected by Butler and Athanasiou: a dispossession can imply a loss of property, self or other propriety, yet is also invokes a release from being possessed by forces external to the integrity of being, or at least to be aware of the pressure placed upon the self by these external factors. Coupled with the notion of the performative, in light of its political agentic capacities, this points toward the postmodern fragmentation of the subject, its shifting identities across malleable time-space constructed through memory. All this occurs within the dimension of the visual multimedia cyberspaces that recuperate the real performances recorded of these poets' readings of their works.

The political effects of these spaces of appearance of performed poetry in activisms, videos, and installations of Machado, Colombino, and Cerón engage non-gendered bodily perspectives and discrete elements of sound, in concert with the word, providing clues for grounding our discussion of poetry in action on transnational social themes and alliances.

As our point of reference will explore how Machado, Colombino and Cerón participated in the United Kingdom's "POETRY PARNASSUS, the UK's largest gathering of the world's poets" from June 26 to July 1, 2012. Held at the Southbank Centre in this self-titled "Festival of the World," it featured live readings, online recordings, poetry installations and handwritten facsimiles of poetic works. Out of this gathering, organized alongside the London Olympics that year, came *The World Record Anthology: International Voices from Southbank Centre's Poetry Parnassus"* (program from the event, 4), featuring 204 poets from the competing Olypmic countries. Sporting events such as these, that host parallel cultural celebrations, grapple with the selection of a representative who will embody the 'national' persona, the best of its artistic 'now.' In this iteration, each poet wrote a poem on handmade paper from around the world, which was bound into a one-off edition for the Poetry Library collection called *The World Record*. The volume, edited by Neil Astley and Anne Selby, was published in a selection collated at the Southbank Centre and published by UK's Bloodaxe Books.

The anthology, which compiled works from every Olympic country, was sold as a souvenir for the festival. In addition to this work in print, e-versions of the poems were performed in a rigorous schedule, alongside innovative sessions and art installations and musical performances. One of the main site installations was an exhibit of the Poetry Parnassus poems, handwritten on paper, streamed across the ceiling on parallel strings in banner formation, over the central auditorium, which created a celebratory setting. Attending receptors could also "watch videos of the poets performing (2012 program, 42) in the original language onsite at the Southbank Centre at various stages, or online from abroad (in recorded video); these appeared without accompanying translations. At the live events, readings by authors were held alongside a program of special themed sessions, such as "The Ministry of Free Speech: We Will Not Be Silent," a free conference of poetry readings, personal narratives and debate about issues faced by poets around the world, and others of regional focus, such as on the Balkans (24) or Europe, the Middle East and Africa (12; 40) and the Pacific Islands. There was no session centered particularly on Latin American authors or on any of the Ibero- or Ibero-American countries. However, Spanish-language poets appeared in several multicultural and themed sessions. For instance, a session titled "Maintenant: A Celebration of the Avant-Garde & The Experimental," on 30 June 2012, had as its focus "poets breaking new ground with form, medium and methodology—the innovators, experimentalists and avant-gardists who make poetry in the 21st century pluralist, dynamic, vibrant and open" (program); Rocío Cerón was among its presenters.

One poet also had an individual presentation, live and recorded for an online series in London, as the official representative for each country. There was a poet from each of the 18 Spanish-speaking Latin American countries in the general daily readings that took place over the course of the festival. The majority of these were women; these included Mirta Rosenberg from Argentina, María Soldedad Quiroga (Bolivia), Alejandra del Río (Chile), Raúl Henao (Colombia), Ana Istarú (Costa Rica), Pedro Pérez Sarduy (Cuba), Chiqui Vicioso (Dominican Republic), Santiago Vizcaíno (Ecuador), Claribel Alegría (representing El Salvador, but who was born in Nicaragua to Salvadorean parents), Giaconda Belli (Nicaragua), Carmen Matute (Guatemala), Mayra Oyuela (Honduras), Lucy Cristina Chau (Panama), Lía Colombino (Paraguay), Victoria Guerrero Peirano (Peru), Vanessa Dross (Puerto Rico), Melisa Machado (Uruguay), and Beverly Pérez Rego (Venezuela), for a total of 15 women and three men. These "Poetry Parnassus Poets" from Spanish America were listed by country in the program. The online components, made available with video recordings of each poet reading against a gallery wall, were also features of the programming and served to create a homogenous background for all of the 204 recordings of the performed texts, uploaded subsequently also on YouTube. The poem for each country was recited by the author in its original language; no translation of the text was provided either as subtitles in the video nor in the accompanying webpage. The distinctiveness, thus, was borne out in the language of each poem, and the reading communicated in the voice and gestural performance of each poet.

ROCÍO CERÓN (MEXICO): "IMPERIO/EMPIRE"

As noted in the program insert for the Poetry Parnassus event, Cerón was born in Mexico City in 1972. Her work is experimental, combining poetry with music, performance and video. Her books of poetry include *Basalto* (2002), *Imperio/Empire* (2009 interdisciplinary bilingual edition), *Tiento* [I Try/I Feel] (Germany, 2011), and *Diorama* (2013), the latter with translation into English by Anna Rosenwong, which was recently awarded the prize for Best Translated Book Award, as announced on 27 May 2015 at BookExpo America in New York City. Cerón's poetry has been widely translated into English, Finnish, French, Swedish and German, and she has performed her work at venues in France, Germany, Sweden and Denmark. Not only is she one of the most prolific and well-known poets in contemporary Mexico, her efforts to interact with other 'world poetries' outside the Americas is evident in her publications record, an aspect also highlighted on her official website: www.rocioceron.com. In 2000, she won the Premio Nacional de Literatura Gilberto Owen for her book *Basalto* published that year, and has served as Editor for Ediciones El billar de Lucrecia.

Rocío Cerón's interventions in London's World Parnassus began on June 27 as part of the session, "Parnassus Cinema: Poetry and Film," the "World Premiere of Kilometer Zero: Poetry, Subversion and Hope." This short film by David Shook, Parnassus Translator in Residence (2012 program, 13), had its world premiere at the event. Its subject matter traced "Equatorial Guinea's media hostile borders to find lost poet Marcelo Ensema Nsang" (program, 13), and was preceded by "two forthcoming film-poetry projects and followed by a Q&A session with David Shook, Rocío Cerón and other Parnassus poets" (13). The languages indicated by the epitaph of this program-page entry for the film showings included English, Spanish, and Isthamus Zapotec, the latter an indigenous language spoken in the isthmus of Oaxaca, Mexico, around the Juchitán, a narrow strip of land bordered by water. For Cerón, past and present coloniality of language and discourse constantly intersect in the ambiguous poetic voice who, at the precipice of an abyss created by absence, memory survives through a process of re-naming the image—or rather, unveiling the History of "One Name" (such as in her work *Imperio*) juxtaposed with efforts to reclaim the body as one site linked to many others. In addition to taking part in the aforementioned special sessions, Cerón delivered an individual reading representing Mexico, as was the basic format for the participation of each author from the 204 countries in this "largest poetry festival ever staged in the UK" (www.southbankcentre.co.uk/poetry-parnassus).

Cerón's Dubbing of "América"

To begin with, then, let us turn to the definition of the Pan American that is first apparent in the represented Mexican author. In Cerón's poems we detect the attempt to dismantle imperial discourse in a multilayered, chaotic style that juxtaposes visual imagery with post-feminist and post-colonial awareness. Through what she terms "expanded poetry," her written verses in print are normally later performed live or recorded with sound, images and music, in which her own voice as a woman with Mexican (D.F.) inflection remains central to the enunciation. As she recites the poem, for her intervention at Poetry Parnassus, her voice reflects the textual grappling with historical past as an aspect of her situated sense of loss. The historical weight of Mexico in particular, but more so of "América" as a construct, proves inescapable. The poetic voice finds refuge in the memory of her deceased father, a shield in the present and trope of the past, often displacing her voice into adopting his as the subject of the poems.

The poem titled "América," originally published in Cerón's Tiento (2010), is angry in tone as the rest of this collection; chosen as her contribution to Parnassus 2012 in London, this poem delineates a restorative stance through a geopolitical viewpoint resting in language, and in the awareness of postcolonial angst as seen through the female body. In an alternate recitation of this work, available in video format on Vimeo and You Tube—which we will contrast afterward— Cerón's voice is rather more expressed in a dramatically superimposed tone, echoing as a voice-over with reverb effects. For the Parnassus version she reads simply, albeit with a heightened tone of address: "Dijeron que era hija del golpe, de los barrios donde los sones son lentos y carraspean las voces, y los toneles de aguardiente se empujan sin trozo de pan." This beginning of the poem that highlights the spoken word, in the first line—"they said"— immediately brings to the fore the challenge: whose story is being told, and what is the genealogy? For If we are to understand that, "they said she was a daughter of the coup, where the sounds are slow and the voices scratch, and casks of moonshine abound…"], we are left awaiting a reversal, or subsequent assertions about who "they" are, and also about who "she" is. The verb in active preterit form, "dijeron," is repeated three times in the text; this reiterated intensity in the plural third person, and in the past, versus the pronouncement over a singular feminine subject, appears threatening in its construal of power relations. The brutal force of the lexicon emphasizes the hostile stance against the "daughter" (of the first line) among them "empujan," in the first clause, and into the next two: "dijeron que era hija desprecio, de esclavas, de amargas noches, de cama entre soldados y cuerpos cobrizos; dijeron que era una mártir"; this insistence could also be read as a vulnerable stance of the victimhood claimed by the undermining force placed against the true character of the "she" described. What arrests the flow of the they said/what she is to be, is found in the next two sets of verb constructions which are set apart in the text not only by dashes but also by cursive format: "—estaba, están equivocados—" ("América," part IV). The implicit poetic voice corrects history. It is not known until the last line of the poem that this subject is the history of a continental divide, whose history Cerón sums up through the succinct list of tropes: "luego le dieron algo de espejos y algo de carne de cerdo, algo de nuevos nombres y nuevos apellidos; le enseñaron el uso de la rueda (ya conocía el cero); casi la mata la fiebre. Y de cada golpe ha salido más fuerte. Como el poema, América es una dura cicatriz en el cuerpo." Body as the site of history is uncontested. However, its appellation into discourse, through naming that historical location as feminine (becoming in effect a 'biosymbol' as per Yépez, 2013), returns the agency of the oppressed within colonialism by reconstruction of that history in the present.

The insistence on "América" as an open wound, echoing Galeano's well-known metaphor of the region's "open veins," reconsiders, remembers at different temporal junctures and from various spaces, this grappling with unresolved postcolonial relations, by personifying the Spanish- speaking aspects of the political divides. The combination of sound, word, image and gesture provide plasticity and dramatism employed in the performed reading combine to create the prose-poem's meaning, but it does so as a form of collage of verses, a palimpsest of trauma. "De cada golpe, ha salido más fuerte," as one of the final verses in the poem, confirms a series of acts that recall past trauma and memory in order to reformulate the information and thereby construct a new "feminine" subject from the echoes. The questionable aspect of this assertion in Cerón's poetry is the usage of a totalizing female subject co-relative for the geo-political space referred to as "América." To what this extent this reversal of the monolith from a patriarchy to a generalized female symbol of victimhood can be salvaged into a new affirmation liberated from the underlying postcolonial effects of oppression and wounding remains un-accessed in this poem. The objective seems to lie, in this reading at least, in the affective tone of resurfacing from which these images emerge, yet there is no solution laid bare other than simply the act of enunciating the revelations.

What Cerón's poem does assert, however, is the doubling of the image of "América/America." The totalizing nature is uncovered here. Heriberto Yépez refers to this as a gendered quality of language, and this dimension is highly evoked in Cerón's poem. Yépez, as another contemporary Mexican writer and cultural critic, also interrogates this notion in his discussion of empire: "Why does woman signify body, psycho-historically? Because the parallel fantasy indicates that male signifies mind. 'Woman' is that which the 'male' unknowns of himself. And vice versa" (2013, 14). Transposed from the individual body to the larger context of history, the connection to Cerón's personification of the victims of imperial projects, in this case generalized as a Latin American plural subject, finds escape from the wounding by grounding itself again in the voice of one female poet. By usurping the power of the word, "Imperio/Empire" is doubled, the other side of the coin now (en)gendered anew through a naming of the crime. No specific heroes, no victims, are signaled. The 'new corpus' is expanded to encompass all wounding to all bodies in space and time, or what Yépez terms "the pseudo-maternal," (19), which Mexico symbolizes, in his view, for the North American. The return to the site of the repression, following this view, is at the same time an assertion that, as Butler and Athanasiou have posited in their term "dispossession," the process to reclaim the possession of the body's lost fragments, is always tied inextricably to the other, and to the self's position vis-à-vis the dominant discourse. The (relational, creative, affective) body, nevertheless, emerges as the key piece in resolving the aporetic nature of the process.

In similar ways, Melisa Machado and Lía Colombino utilize sound, either in reciting on video, or by combining their voice with music and other arts, to posit ambiguity in the subject via expression through language, on one hand, and the authority of the body on the other. They each only appeared once in the overall series of readings, rather than in any of the special workshops or sessions at Parnassus 2012 such as Cerón did, yet they confirm the importance this exposure had on the availability of their works to new audiences. As all the authors selected for the Poetry Parnassus festival did, the poets stood against a white gallery wall with drawings and before the camera to read their texts for the video recording, rendering evident this aspect of the written as the source of their word. This type of performance by reading a text privileges the voice and the body's stance before a quiet listener; it becomes a shared form of solitude. We will also examine some of their other works in live performance that are recorded and available in video online.

MELISA MACHADO (URUGUAY): "EL CANTO ROJO"

Born in the central region of Uruguay in the district of Durazno in 1966, Melisa Machado works as a physical therapist, art consultant, journalist, performer and dancer, and teaches creative writing at ORT University in Uruguay. In 2009 she was awarded a CUNY grant, and in 2012 another from FEFCA of the Ministry of Culture of the Uruguayan Government. She has participated in various international poetry festivals, including Granada (Nicaragua), Mexico City and London. She is one of the most recognized poets from the country as evidenced in academic studies taking place of her work abroad, especially in the United States. *Ritual[e]s* (Montevideo, 2011) collects five books of her poetry including *Adarga* (2000), *Jamba de Flores Negras* (2006) and *Marjal* (2008). She recently published a second book of poems titled *El canto rojo* (2013).

Her short stories, as well as her poems, have been included in anthologies such as *El Amplio Jardín* (published by the Colombian embassy and Ministry of Education, 2005) and *Nada es igual después de la poesía: cincuenta poetas uruguayos del medio siglo* (Ministry of Education and Archivo General de la Nación, 2005)" (2012 program insert). In May 2008, her poem "Alojaba un cachorro de hombre," was included in the recital "Mujeres en mi voz," organized by Andrés Stagnaro, with dramatization by Raquel Diana. At the time of her participation in UK's Poetry Parnassus, she was "writing a book about Uruguayan artist, Marcelo Legrand, and writing articles for culture magazine Dossier on dance, literature and plastic arts" (insert, 2012). Her work has been translated into English and Swedish.

Melisa Machado's recorded reading in video format of selections from her book *Marjal* for the Olympic Poetry Parnassus inscribes in the poetic voice an aspect of the body as singular presence in a shifting outward locale, but one rooted in an inner animalistic core. The depiction of a dangerous environment in which the subject finds itself is the reason it must access a wider state of consciousness beyond that space in order to survive.

For this aspect Machado activates a secondary referencing level to the historicity and cultural milieu of its origins, one that reaches into the roots and marrow of things... As she writes in the first untitled poem of her book *Marjal,* collected in *Rituales*: "El hueso del desgarro no es el hueso / del abismo. Es tu hueso, tu cuchillo. / Ardamos, polvo de huesos" ("*Marjal*," 2011, 137) (The bone of the searing rupture is not the bone of the abyss. It is your bone, your blade. Let us burn, dust of bones.) These opening lines reach into a doubling, as we saw in Cerón's "América," a double negation: what is it not. It is not the bone that has been torn, or ripped apart from the body to be thrown into an abyss; it is part of your body.

The singular bone then transforms into a plural image of burning, with its multiple allusion across historical times of war, censorship, torture, and yet does it also contain a positive connotation? In the next and final line of this opening four-verse poem, the plural imperative to own the fire-driven action is connected to the affective state of loving the "cachorro" or the cub of the beast, the one of our choosing: "Bien amado sea el cachorro de bestia que elegimos" (Machado, 2011, 137) (Let the cub of our chosen beast be loved). The poetic voice's pronouncement, vehiculized in the use of the subjunctive form of the imperative meaning, "Bien amado sea," or let it be loved so well, ushers in an undertone typically found of commandments of Biblical authority. These resonances reappear at the end of "*Marjal*," and in them I find comparative forms in Colombino's poem "El costado," in particular to the way the human and post-human call upon the pre-human to remember and gather lost fragments of the subject's experiences.

Machado's reading of the first eight her poems from *Marjal* at the Poetry Parnassus makes evident an "animalistic" perception of the body, a focus on its sovereignty as a locus of meaning that is very relevant in the context of a sporting event. The body as "bête machine" on the one hand, contrasts with the sensibility or dominion of the cultural on the other. The oral performance of the poem additionally brings an attunement with alliterative repetitions (of the 'rr' for eg. In "desgarro" and "cachorro"), the biology of the body merged with interior and exterior feeling. This is further filtered through an affective state of inquiry through sensation, and the situationality of self and other. The other, however, is not necessarily the interlocutor of a dialogue on themes, but rather an invited participant in a grounding work of sensorial awareness. The ideas of the poem flow through its imagery of "animal" (verses 6 and 27), "hocico voraz" (verse 9), and "cachorro" (verse 4), or "bestia" (verses 5 and 30), and fauna in "todo jazmín" (title and verse 8); some could be either for the human or non-human such as "hueso" (verse 1), "lenguas" (versee 6), "mandíbulas" (verse 10), "lomo" (verse 11). Others are purely human: "cabellos" (verse 28), "manos" (verse 25) (*Rituales*, 2011).

There is something about this correlation in the objectification of one's own body as animal, beast and hairy creature that apparently belies an awareness of the postcolonial undercurrent, on one hand, and a cybernetic disconnect from the physical, on the other. That is, the body is encumbering in its density and fixity in time and space. Self-determination, thus, is first a reckoning with the past that escapes any agentic control by the individual subject. Its body is subjugated to the categorization of lower natures and vulnerabilities that cyber-worlds would seek to eradicate or blur. The old dichotomy *barbarie/civilización* bears threatening undertones as a remnant of the past value system with its roots in the present state of being-ness in the body.

We could link this with political divides by suggesting tangentially that it brings to mind previous themes, hiding the colonialist idealization of the language of identity (laying bare the linguistic strains upon the body's hypervalent presences in various levels at once; that is, the surplus of being that is incapable of being expressed only in existing verbal language and that meaning that seeks expression through other means, such as poetry, sound, music, gesture and movement). How to circumvent these in language, through poetic verse, but without abandoning the body's rite of passage as an inheritor of its history, and as the vehicle for participating in the social world in shared speech patterns?

Closely tied to this subterranean critique of colonialist discourse and linguistic structures is the representation of the landscape in Machado's work. As in the other poets here studied, and for example in previous generations of writers, Mario Vargas Llosa's assessment of the lingering inheritance of colonialisms still echoes. In the dominant discourse of the nation and in a broader representation of national identity for which natural symbols were put in play into a specific imaginary, the idealization of the indigenous, coupled with a romantic notion of the land and its characteristics representing a culture, now break down into subsets of time, discourse and image as they are reverted to a beastly realm. The spatialization in verses 7-8 of Machado's "Jamba"—or threshold, doorway, made of black flowers, creates a binary that rests on the natural landscape. The rest of the poem makes mention of another element of floral imagery—"La piel toda escamas, toda jazmín, fuego" —placing at the fore the sensorial nature and the tactile awareness of the body's presence in its transformations.

As Tobias Menely argues in *The Animal Claim: Sensibility and the Creaturely Voice*, "The capacity to vocalize a claim to moral consideration is creaturely, even if the responsibility for such claims is definitely human. […] While conventional signs facilitate abstract cognition, natural signs 'give force and energy to language' (96-97). Great orators and poets, according to Reid, recover a communicative power that has been 'unlearned' in the learning of culture. (35). Menely argues for the "remediation [of the natural sign] in poetic language, print, and political debate" (35), and examines "implications of the sensibility's model" (35).

The rising from the ashes evoked in the title of Machado's poem for Poetry Parnassus 2012, manifests a metamorphosis. The first phase into which her text descends—first with reference to the "scaly" nature of the skin, a type of pre-human, or beastly, reptilian, aquatic creature—finally ascends toward a celestial realm. There the sin is pardoned by a winged emissary or "velludo animal…voló" ("Marjal," 2011, 141) (the hairy animal flew) cited at the end of her recited verses. The sensuality of the body echoes the animalistic comparisons in its relationship with the beastly form.

These contain both sensual and threatening characteristics, evident in "las mandíbulas tajantes" and "la sedosa piel de lomo" (second and third verses of poema "II," 139) as well as referencs to the "hocico" (snout) (poem "II," 139), "lengua bífida" (forked tongue) and "de quijada presta"(ready jaw) (both of the latter in poem "III" of "*Marjal*," 139); these images reference the mouth of the animal, focusing on its raw agression. By the end of the poem the focus reaches the extremities (evident in the simile of the hands as birds of sweet crumbs of bread), and the poetic view shifts to a surprising new relationship with the subject (as we saw above in the last verse: "Voló hacia mí," or 'It flew to me.') We should also mention the foundational function of this last animal figure, echoing the architectural space of the encounter: "Elveeludo animal dejó / cimiente" (poem "VI, 140) "(The hairy animal it laid the foundation). The presence in poem "V" of hands that are like birds of "migas dulces" (sweet crumbs) could imply, at least to this reader, a movement of the body in its metaphoric dance between the relational nature and the hunger for freedom and for pleasure.

In a video interview in September 2012, Uruguayan researcher Paola Gallo considers the reference to fruit in the other parts of this larger seventeen-part work "Jambas de flores negras," with its insistences on the sour taste or rasping texture of peaches, for instance, as encapsulating a transgressive, raw eroticism of the body. Furthermore, the apparent "desorden" that characterizes Machado's style, as Gallo believes, points to a deeper movement of meaning that is liberating and connects on a sensorial level. Yet these seem to confound the poetic voice, interrogating the subject through the body, as it seeks its way out of the maze of perceptions. Built by discourse that escapes intellectual decoding, the poem becomes the site of questioning via the body, a release beyond normative stances that makes any communicative stance an uneasy one, heightened by implicit threats of historical valences hidden in the dangerous terrain of language.

In a 2014 interview for *Revista Bla* (Juan Andrés Ferreira), Machado responded to a question about poetry's contemporary function. Confessing that this question arose for her only after the Parnassus participation, Machado responds by positing the oral components of poetry as its greatest strengths:

> It always astounds me that poetry does not sell, that publishing houses do not publish it, or that bookstores place it in the most hidden places on their shelves, and yet poetry is capable of uniting people from across the world, and governments and institutions invest financially in it. It is always continually read in clubs and pubs. There is a flagrant contradiction in this. I think that poetry should return to its initial vehicle: the voice, sound. A return to orality, to the troubadours. It should be spoken, rapped, sung. (2013)

The tension between the oral and print components of poetry is evident here as well. Without wishing to discard either side of the generic divide, Machado is nevertheless keenly aware of the ability of the oral performance of poetry to reach audiences. In response to Ferreira's interview question about how she defines poetry, Machado answers: "No la definiría, pero si no tengo más remedio diría que es un juego al que no puedo negarme porque se me impone desde un lugar arquetípico y como tal, es inconciente y me posee" (ibid) (I would not define it, yet if pressed to do so I'd say it's a game I can't deny myself because it imposes itself on me from an archetypal place and as such, it's unconscious and it possesses me).

Melisa Machado's interest in the Eastern philosophies of writing with (and from) the body is an attempt to circumvent mental strategies learned in submission to external systems of education and social settings. As per Lyotard in the defining of the postmodern condition, Machado attempts to invoke "the unpresentable in the presentation itself, that which refuses the consolation of correct forms, refuses the consensus of taste permitting a common experience of nostalgia for the impossible, and inquires into new presentations—not to take pleasure in them, but to better produce the feeling that there is something unpresentable" (74). That is, through the body we seek that which cannot be accessed in conventional language, returning the abstracted body in the text, to the sensual body as text. Beyond this there is the Latin American reality that is at the heart of the "unpresentable" or the "crisis of representation" that Lyotard theorized.

Poetry, Tango, Spoken Word

As a counterpoint and to expand what we have discussed thus far with regard to Melisa Machado's poetry, I would like to now turn to an examination of another of her online video recordings. One of the most incisive in its approach to performativity via the use of staging, lighting and sound production has been her recitations/readings of *El canto rojo*, performed and filmed in association with Chilean Cristóbal Severín Garcés, who resides in Montevideo and created the visual effects, as well as Urugayan Pablo Bonilla, who composed the music for the piece. The performance served as the focal point for the launch of the book with the same title. The event was presented as a "poetic concert" (review of the piece, 2013) on May 23, 2013 at the Centro Cultural de España in Montevideo.

The performance included negan with the sound of electronic music. A foreboding staccato sound introduced the audience to a darkened stage. Slowly one yellow-white stage light spotlighted a hand holding a book, the face of the poet remaining in shadow, while the sound of a bandoneón (a small concertina type accordion typically associated with the tango) joined the initial electronic piano melody. Machado's voice readi from the book while the screen displayed a digital form of the title CANTO ROJO is red capital letters: "La prosperidad de mi lengua. Los animales blancos. Los animales negros" (The prosperity of my tongue. White animals. Black animals) [0:19–0:29]. At this point the poet's name appears in digital type on the screen, to the left of her position at the centre of the stage/screen. This type was smaller than the previous titutar format, and in white capital letters instead. She continued: "Los líquidos venenosos del agua límpida. La resurección de la carne. La resurrección en todas sus formas. El pecado" (The venomous liquids of the limpid wáter. The resurrection of the flesh. Resurrection in all its forms. Sin) [0:30–0:43].

In the next scene, as the music of the bandoneón increased its amplification, Machado's reading was accompanied by the projection of words on a large screen behind her. Green computer type flowed across the background as if revealed through clouds. These were verses of her poems in print typeface as well as script form; one of the most evident phrases was "…que ama al hermano, q…" (who loves his/her brother, q). During this section, Machado recited verses from the book she held; at this point more stage lighting made her standing body more visible to the audience: "Cubrí su cuerpo con flores y otras hierbas. Luego de cuatro semanas de navegar por tierra. Macerados, nos dejábamos acunar por la marea" (I covered his/her body with flowers and other herbs. After four weeks of navigating on land, macerated, we let ourselves be rocked by the tide) [0:47–0:43].

These verses usher in the flow of blue lights, in swirling shapes, letters and mysterious symbols that spill into words, on the screen behind Machado [0:51–1:01]. "Bendito sea este vientre," Machado continued, "el estoque, su dulzura y su armadura" (Blessed be this womb, the sword[14], its sweetness and armor) [1:03–1:09]. A movement of the camera opens and then waits on a wider camera angle which now reveals Machado's body almost in its entirety (except for the lower portions of her legs). She stood, dressed in black trousers and a three-quarter length long-sleeved black t-shirt. Her body created a tall shadow straight above her as it eclipsed some of the handwritten words in light blue ink projected on the navy toned screen behind her.

The rest of the stage to the right was in black. To stage left there was a doubling of the image of her hands holding the book from which she read. She paused to look straight at the camera, that is the audience in front of her. The camera focused obliquely from the left of the screen on her torso and face, and the words projected echo what she has just read. Turning the page, she continued. Circular blue lights then turned into vertical streams and the poet's verses continue after a brief pause in which the music is louder, then subsided to the sound of her voice: "El invierno en la panza de los pájaros. El frío en el pan humeante y tu lengua en la fiebre. He aquí la lengua desatada al borde de los dientes. La turba, el pantano, la terraplen. El declive solar, el pelo como manta, el lado más sombrío de la luna" (Winter in the belly of birds. Cold on steaming bread and your feverish tongue. Here I have the loose tongue at the edge of my teeth. The peat, the marsh, the embankment. The solar slope, hair like a blanket, the darker side of the moon) [1:17–1:44]. During the reading of these verses, the screen expanded the movement and size of the spirals, elongating their shape, still in blue tones. The last visual image resembled a net hanging over Machado's upper body, becoming spheric as it disappeared from view. The bandoneón and undercurrent of electronic percussive sounds emoted the slow yet disturbing tone of the piece.

After this midway point in the performance a major visual and sonoric shift has occured. The intensity of the bandoneón lifted, it has played increasing staccato higher pitched notes, while the colour of the entire background shifted to red. Additional percussion produced electronically changes the dynamic of the musical accompaniment. More upbeat, quicker paced, it escorted the image on the screen of a spinning red circle with white dots on the left [1:45–1:510]; a shadow of Machado appeared, opposite on the screen to the right, dancing against a red circle projected behind her [1:51–1:58]. Machado's voice was heard with reverb effects the screen expanded with star-like white lights against the jet-black background.

---

[14] This is a type of narrow sword, or rapier, normally used in bullfighting and that only wounds at the point.

E-Poetry: Videopoetry, Text, Aurality and Music

The red circle remained on stage right, with the dancing shadow continuously moving across it in various fluid steps. The verses in this portion of the performance change to a more sensual theme: "Pienso en la fruta morada, sabrosa como agua de hibiscos, agua de Jamaica, de Jaramillo. Tengo la lengua afilada como un estilete. Un ojo que ve, y otro que no. Y la boca del volcán sujeta a mis palabras. Salen de mí, vocales rojas, mientras oprimo esta ciudad entre los muslos. Abierta, duermo hacia el silencio. (I think about purple fruit, savory like hibiscus water, hibiscus tea, of Jaramillo. My tongue is sharp like a stylus. One eyes that sees, the other does not. And the mouth of the volcano holds on to my words. They arise from me, red vowels, as I crush this city in my thighs. Open, I sleep toward the silence) [1:56–2:33]. Amidst the red tonality that has predominated the scene against which a dancing shadow moves, other tonalities of evergreen and bright yellow, for example, add dimension in wedge and sun shaped colour forms. Across this visual scape, the music has maintained its dynamic percussive persistence until the end of the performance. The last verse is read by Machado with no music, as if to punctuate the final word: "silence".

At first glance, the tongue, the insistence on Biblical resonances (sin; beatitudes: Blessed be; transmutations and resurrections) are configured in "El canto rojo" against the River Plate cultural references of the tango and the visual scape of a city that Machado never names but that we can infer is Montevideo. The music provides the chronotope, and submerges the verses in another sphere of meaning (pun intended). The "redness" of the shift at the performance's hallway point, coincides with the change in the discursive tone of the poem. Whereas it had begun very much like *Marjal* in listing of an animalistic body as aggressive, dangerous, it has by the middle succumbed to a pleasure principle encapsuled in the image of the purple fruit and the flavourful waters. Redepmtion has thus appeared again here, as in Marjal; introduced by the beastly creature, the poetic first-person voice lets the rhythm of the body, its sensations and movements, overcome the thinking self. The subjective voice is empowered over the environment, a fact highlighted by the red tones and solitary dance moves in focus. Machado's reading stance is no longer visible by that point. The body itself seems speak through Machado's voice heard now, as mentioned, with reverb effect, which creates a sense of distance and all-pervasive presence simultaneously.

In addition, the affirmation of strength of the self over the city, the overturning of oppression that makes the city now succumb to her thighs and to her red vowels, is amplified by the increasing speed with which the dancing shadow body is seen to move across the screen. In its final verses, Machado's poem exerts its pressure from that core of embodied meaning, as if the blood path of the internal self now sees everything as subject to its dominion. The vowels, the open sounds of language that create reality and meaning, are red as she speaks; therefore implied here, perhaps in not only the militant stance, but also a passionate break with lifelessness, or with that which is opposed to life. As the theme of resurrection opened the piece, it is potent that the final openness of the subject, which then transforms into complete silence, would reinforce that awe before its own scope, power and creative ease that stems from sleep. The contrapuntal nature of the piece reflects the duality that dissolves self from other. In the end, the self is the only other on stage. From the darkness of conflict (dark side of the moon, the black and white animals, the night and day shades of light, the venom) is birthed ("blessed be this womb") from sweetness and harshness (armour, sword). The natural landscape cocoons and cuddles the self (peat, embankment, blanket) until it blossoms forth in fruitfulness.

By tracing the links of these images and new media representations of the non-material mirrored in the body and the landscape, the past, present and future connect across the geographical spaces of Uruguay and the Americas, and link us in a common humanity's hope for resurrecting a renewed respect for the sense of place and self. In these works the future is envisioned as a return to ancient stories whereby the use of sound and imagery are instrumental in depicting tacit knowledge. By tracing the links of these images and new media representations of the non-material mirrored in the body and the landscape, these works make us aware of the relationship of land and self as "an infinite refrain" (Nagam 92). As in Machado's fifth book of poetry, *Marjal*, collected in her volume *Rituales* and performed in her videos, *El canto rojo*, shares references to imagery of bone, blood memory, the animal self's access to deep knowledge, and a recognition of the flow in the natural landscape that is not concrete, but in flux; the flows reflects its living beingness and its connection to humanity.

LÍA COLOMBINO (PARAGUAY): *PROYECTO AURICULAR*

In contrast, Lía Colombino's work moves against the socially transgressive nature of the body's desires and seeks rather reconciliation with, or reconfiguration of, its nestled habitat beyond the need for social connection. It appears to return hermetically to self as refuge, and to the nature of the body as a way out of communicational impasses.

Colombino (1974-), a native of Asunción, is the founder of the cultural collective *Ediciones de la Ura*. She coordinates two writing workshops in Paraguay, one of which is part of the National University's *Instituto Superior de Arte* official curriculum. She worked in radio for the program "Al Filo de la Palabra" (Radio FM La Tribu) in Buenos Aires in 1997. Her books include *Las cavidades ausentes* (2000), *Tierra de Secano* (2001), *Proyecto Auricular* (an audio book with musician Javier Palma, 2006) and (lupa) (2009). She has taken part in several festivals in Latin America, most recently in Nicaragua, Chile and Cuba (2012 program insert). She is also a museologist and current director of the *Museo del Barro* in Paraguay. In May 2015 she was asked to curate the exhibition "Chaco Ra'anga," organized by the *Red de Centros Culturales de la Agencia de Cooperación Internacional para el Desarrollo* (AECID). This has involved traversing the Gran Chaco with a group of artists and scientists to bring attention for the need of greater commitment to sustainable development. Her emphasis on collective efforts, and on the connection to geographic spaces of identity and agency, recall Cerón's drive to heal the "body" of "América" by adopting the plural in the poetic voice.

In "El costado," read by Colombino at the Southbank Centre's Poetry Parnassus, we see an initial allusion, in the title, to the side: could it be interpreted as that of the Biblical Adam? If so, we could follow this line of questioning in the text. On the other hand, subsequently in the text, a mythological reference to the "cíclope," the one-eyed monster of the Titan from Greek mythology, such as Atlas who bears the weight of the sky on his shoulders, brings a heightened awareness of the urge for and decomposition of uneasy symbiosis, one that stems from irreconcilable aspects of the self. The disharmony between the body and surrounding forces joins with a sense of connection to the earth; together, this uneasy process becomes a means for counteracting the perceived dangers posited by the monster and the physical world. Both mythical aspects, the Judeo-Christian and the ancient Greek, focus upon the imaging faculty and its role in causing separation between the human and its connection to source.

The reference to Adam, ensuing from the title's allusion to the creation of woman from the side of the first man, recalls the dominion that he had been given over all creatures and the world. According to the Book of Genesis, God created first the animals (Gen.1: 20-25), after having made the world and its natural environment, including light, sky, water (seas and rivers), earth (plants, fruits, vegetation, seed, seasons, moon and sun (Gen. 1: 1-19). Following the "creatures of the sea" and birds (verse 20), and "wild animals of the earth," God then created "humankind in his image" (Genesis 1: 26); this imaging aspect is repeated and explained in subsequent verses: "in the image of God he created them; male and female he created them (Gen. 1: 27). Nevertheless, in the second account of creation, in Book 2 of Genesis, this chronology is not identical. It rather highlight's the predominance of "Adam" and his central role in naming God's creation: "In the day that the Lord God made the earth and the heavens, when no plant of the field was yet in the earth and no herb of the field had yet sprung up—for the Lord God had not caused it to rain upon the earth, and there was no one to till the ground; but a stream would rise from the earth, and water the whole face of the ground—then the Lord God formed man from the dust of the ground, and breather into his nostrils the breath of life; and the man became a living being" (Gen. 2: 4-7). Woman appears at the end of this chapter: "Then the Lord God said: 'It is not good that the man should be alone; I will make him a helper as his partner.' So out of the ground the Lord God formed every animal of the field and every bird of the air, and brought them to the man to see what he would call them" (Gen. 2: 18-19).

The naming of the animals, as Menely discusses in *The Animal Claim*, represents this emphasis of the idealization of the other creatures that immediately succumb to the power of Adam's words. This dominion proclaimed via fiat ordered by God clearly identifies the order of things: man, beasts, and the woman follows only after the company of animals proves insufficient in the realm of creation's chronology: "The man gave names to all cattle, and to the birds of the air, and to every animal of the field; but for the man there was not found a helper as his partner. So the Lord God caused a deep sleep to fall upon the man, and he slept; then he took one of his ribs and closed up its place with flesh. And the rib that the Lord God had taken from the man he made into a woman and brought her to the man" (Gen. 2: 20-22). What ensues is the reaffirmation of utterance as a male imperative in the creation process, and the masculine word as following in the line of God's granted authority on earth: "Then the man said, 'This at last is bone of my bones / and flesh of my flesh; / this one shall be called / Woman, / for out of Man this one was taken'" (Gen. 2: 23).

Colombino's selected poem for Paraguay's entry in the 2012 Poetry Parnassus posits the feminine voice as an embedded "co-body" (to borrow a term from Yépez, 21), that is, as a derivative or shadow of man. Woman is "dispossessed" from the body of the man, to be claimed by man as helper for his purposes. This one step removal from the earth also denotes a distance from the center of dominion agency. Also key is that the woman first speaks in the Bible only in dialogue with the serpent, to explain the decree from God of what fruits were to be eaten in the garden. She falls prey to the serpent's fabrication, the antithesis of the God decree of life and death, and ushers in the age of sin and shame of nakedness. When God returns to find that this has occurred, he directs his question to the man: "But the Lord God called to the man, and said to him, 'Where are you? (Gen. 3: 9). The spatial implication is one of hiding, transgression and shame; when Adam comes out he confesses his fear and God speaks to him: "Who told you that you were naked?" Have you eaten from the tree of which I commanded you not to eat? The man said, 'The woman whom you gave to be with me, she gave me the fruit from the tree, and I ate.' Then the Lord said to the woman, 'What is this that you have done?' The woman said, 'The serpent tricked me, and I ate' " (Gen. 3: 11-13). The spiritual considerations in theology about the fallout from this notion of original sin is well-known, yet it bears emphasizing that the forms of address and the naming processes embedded in this religious text highlight the position of the body as wound or as dangerous, as animalistic. It forms the crux of the matter in Menely's argument for resituating our notions of the "animal claim" vis-à-vis discursive and poetics today, and which informs my interpretation of the three women poets under discussion here. As the serpent is able to outwit Eve (who is so named only in verse 20, after the punishment is ordained for the sin), the man blames both God, for having created the woman, and the woman, for his only crime was to trust her, his need of her being the cause of this fall from grace. This female connection to the animalistic sphere bears further examination.

In Colombino's poem, chosen as representative of Paraguay at the largest sports event in the world, this grants it an unusual extra-territorial power to enunciate the wounding of empire in conjunction with that of the subjugated female voice/body, alongside other co-bodies who are shadows within the imperial design (such as the doubly repressed indigenous body). "El costado" or "The Side" also plays neatly into a double entendre of politics as a sporting analogy, off side or side of a field, that can either be a cunning (non-transparent) play or a missed goal (penalty). With these and especially with the Biblical allusions in mind from the onset of the text, the first verb of the poem "Cargo" denotes the weight of the world, or the burdening felt by the poetic voice's dealings with its natural surroundings. The subject "I" grapples with the elements—windstorm, cloud—that could be seen as metaphors of voicings (breath and vocal chords) or of the churnings of the mind, among other possible tropes of perception, communication and conceptualization of the world through these natural symbols. Carrying this burden, the poetic voice responds to the challenge by adjusting the cloud over the Cyclops' head. This creature is a terrifying giant, the most famous of whom is Homer's Polyphemus, son of Poseidon in Greek cosmology. This connection to the god of the sea provides us with additional links of the implied reference to aquatic symbolism, perhaps an allusion to the subconscious realms, and the connection between sea and air in generating storms and clouds. Poseidon is also known for his agonistic nature.

The next verb construction in the poem, "I dream" (verse 3) is a departure from the embattled opening scenes. The voicing of this verb is left adrift in an open-ended sentence. It is followed in verse 4 by a longer sentence in which the rupture with language comes to the fore after dreaming: "Rompo palabras ajenas y me pueblo." By breaking words that are foreign to itself, the poetic voice becomes a self-generated plurality, as we see in the unusual reflexive form of the verb "poblar"—to populate onself—that Colombino employs here. But rather than as expansionism, the emphasis remains on the interiority of the process, as we witness in the next verse in which the lyrical first person 'touches the fingers of her breath,' thereby merging the external and internal bodies. Nevertheless, the utterance recalls the Biblical pronouncement to "be fruitful and multiply" and the locus of the life-giving impulse in the breath.

The constant movement or restless rustling evident in Colombino's texts is described by the poet herself as the need for text to be "rubbed together" in order to "generate some spark" (interview on Southbank Centre website accompanying the listing for her poetry). Rather than emphasize the sounds of the words, through alliterations and rhythmic juxtapositions as in Machado, nor through prose-like flows of consciousness and antagonisms with the passing of time as in Cerón, Colombino's poetic voice is alert to the movements and (re)positionings of the body itself, a verbal expression of dance that sounds out presence.

For this Paraguayan-born poet, hypertext is a paradigm of postcolonial angst, whereby the impossibility for staticity and stability of the subject vis-à-vis its spaces threatens, as environmental catastrophes and the traumatic effects of political crises become membranes through which the body must pass. The tactile approach renders each reaction a form of survival against the anxiety of entropic disintegration: "Yo toco los dedos del aliento" and "en el fondo." The animal is 'excavates' and 'buries' at the same time. The poetic voice reveals this in the verb "cavar"—"Yo cavo en el fondo /// mi animal'"—in lines spaced openly, from the twelfth, which posits the action of excavating, passing through two spaces of empty lines, that spill into the final one: " mi animal." Taken from, and borne in the 'depths,' the action of creating the animal figure implies a delving into (literally this implies 'digging,' or figuratively speaking, 'meditating profoundly'); it could also denote other meanings as in 'planting' or 'hoeing' for reaping a harvest.

The grounding activity is shaped by the same self, identified with the poetic voice, which grapples with harnessing the impending forces of the windstorm described in the initial segment of the poem. Similar to the subject in Machado's "*Marjal*," she awaits the blow: "Hambre tensa: zarpazo" (verse 4, poema "V" of "*Marjal*," 2011, 140). As in Machado's poetic voice, in Colombino's poem the blows from the wind (or the "zarpazo" of Machado's poem, alluding to a lashing out or blow as part of a beating, is normally attributed to animal attacks) compete with the desire for natural utopias that surface periodically in her imagery, especially in the metaphors of the flora and fauna of Paraguay. On the other hand, the element of sin implied in the title of Colombino's poem, "El costado," becomes outright absolution in Machado's "*Marjal*" thanks to the animal voice in poems "I" to "VI" (2011, 139-141) of the collection. At the end of poem "I" (139), the animal is worn out and described from the inside out, what it drinks, what it looks like. Certain beasts appear, as well as creatures whose actions are compared to the winds in poema "V" (140); a tiger (poema "III," verse 4, 139); an avian allusion in poem "V" (verse 4, 140) and "VI" (verse 5, 141), and a 'hairy animal' in the first verse of poem "VI" (140). These images lead to the poem's powerful conclusion: the gluttonous beast flies to the first person subject (again, as in the case of Colombino's poem, of unknown gender) and declares the absolution from the past: "Voló hacia mí y dijo: 'será limpio tu pecado'." (poem "VI," verses 5–6, 141) (It flew to me and said: 'Your sin will be forgiven'.) The beast absolves the first person subject of its sin. It was its home of choosing from the start of the poem: is this, then, self-absolution? Is the animal a representation of the double self, the other voice, that of the inner repression which has been cut off from the self's constructed social image? Where does the relational force of the animalistic figure reside in the text? As Machado performs the sounds of the poem, the quiet rendering of the enunciation underscores this internal questioning, and a muted assumption of responsibility.

While in Cerón's *Imperio* we saw the fusion of plasticity, sound, word, image and gesture as inseparable megaliths of power, interspersed with the appearance of an individual making its way through the maze of war imagery of various epochs, in Colombino's work sound becomes disjointed like broken pieces reassembled in a different type of chaos, that of shards of perception. In Cerón, a collage of oscillating images evoke strength of recuperation; in Colombino it implies solitude and isolation, while at the same time it affirms a collectivity through poetic affiliations in sound. The animal in Machado and Colombino's texts speaks but through sensations and pulsations, the Barthesian grain of the voice left to do it's bidding on us, in all its fragility, recomposed repeatedly in subjective positionings.

In "El costado," Colombino's poetic voice expresses the experience of a subject under the strain of its bodily existence. The weight of this sensorial ontology is borne in the verb "cargo" which initiates the text, as it struggles under the pressure of "el vendaval," precisely because of its connection to the earthly bearings. The second line of the poem expands this allusion metaphorically into the attempt by the subject to take dominion over the windstorm, perhaps created by the one-eyed beast: "Cargo con el vendaval / Yo ajusto la nube sobre la cabeza del cíclope / Yo sueño / Rompo palabras ajenas y me pueblo / Yo toco los dedos del aliento / Sí / Yo" (verses 2-7). The seeming impossibility of carrying a storm of air captures the sense of utter monumentality of the effort made by the subject. It reaches for the sky to adjust the head of the Cyclops to point toward a desire to undermine unidirectional, single-minded monstrous oppression, in this case by a one-eyed giant (representative of a race of fallen angels in the Biblical tradition, and of pagan gods' offspring in the Greco-Roman one) and by extension this is connected to the male symbol of Adam as a son of patriarchy.

The subject never exposes itself as a feminine voice (in the text, that is, for in the enunciation it is evidently though implicitly so); there is no grammatical indication for it. On the contrary, the ambiguity and constant regeneration of the subject by its own creation, is further expanded in the focus on the voice as disparate, associated with the body as "my animal," as we can appreciate in the final strophes of the poem: "Yo / que cargo la voz de mí / que me inauguro y me dilapido / y que abismo la sílaba hacia un mar" (verses 7-10). The flow-through from the previous verses cited above increase not only the unbearable weight of this process undertaken by the subject, but also the methods by which it imagines its escape through transforming the wind of oppressive pressure and influence on the body, to a vocalization and imagination of the first person subject who takes control of the abyss ("y que abismo la sílaba...") to a reformulating in the largest body of water ("...hacia el mar"). The play on creation through language adopts a sensual turn here, without abandoning a sense of threatening and impending danger, as evidenced in the use of "abismo" and the mysterious and profound direction "hacia el mar." The final verses of the poem, separated by white space on the printed page, and enunciated with greater pause and alacrity by Colombino in her rendition of this poem for Poetry Parnassus in London 2012, emphasize the purpose of the exercise described previously in the text: "Yo cavo en el fondo /// mi animal" (verses 11-12). The spatialization of the "fondo" or depth from which the natural self emerges is attained by removing sediments of time, digging up the bones to sing them into new life. The gestation into flesh, the awareness of bodily sense and its agency, must precede its articulation into the naming of the side to which one belongs. What is known is merely the reverse: the covering under which lies the repossessed word.

Consequently, the three aspects of (1) naming, (2) rejoining of the side to the whole, and (3) finding a link between the creaturely voice and the language of empire (that which resides in inherited systems of discourse, power relations and social structures) reflect the 'uneven postmodernity' that Beverly and Oviedo have argued must take into account Latin America's heterogeneity (4), one that preceded the encounter with European colonialism. By presenting "El costado" at Poetry Parnassus' Olympic event, Colombino does not directly address the past or present of Paraguay in abstract historical terms within the text. She, rather, hinges the theme of the body, its side, onto her attempt to master the foreign (in "ajenas" the meaning can mean both politically and culturally foreign but also alien, strange or belonging to another), which she must first break a priori to the construction of pluralizing herself ("y me pueblo"). In denouncing the dispossession of alienating words, she can in turn repossess the parts of herself formerly claimed by others. The analogy to the cultural is evident in the use of "pueblo." Interesting as well that as a verb it returns agency to the voice, an act consolidated by the affirmation that follows ("Sí / Yo"), as if expecting a doubtful response, rebelliousness in the face of external (and internal?) incredulity at the ability to achieve its objective. The implied dialogic function of the affirmation underscores the stability of the subject even as it traverses into plurality, even as, at the end of the poem, it shifts from the human into animal: "Yo cavo en el fondo / mi animal" (verses 11-12). In a study of Butler and Athanasious performatives, Zeynet Gambetti explains:

> It is because the dispossessed are marked by and bear the burden of 'injurious and unjust genealogies' (99) that Butler and Athanasiou believe vulnerability enables claims of self-determination instead of disabling them. The act of refusing the proper place to which a body is assigned within social structures brings a political subject into existence. The subject thus produced is an effect of the corporeal exercise of a right that does not exist or that is

> extralegal, outside the matrices of intelligibility and normativity. As such, 'performativity works within precarity and against its differential allocation' (101). Street politics in the form of defiance of authority, resistance, and bodily assembly are exposures to vulnerability that simultaneously reject the conditions of dispossession that bodies are differentially made to endure. (Gambetti 257)

Colombino has published other works of poetry, such as "Paraguay en cinco poemas" in her book *Las cavidades ausentes* (2000), yet she did not select one of those to feature at Poetry Parnassus in 2012. Nevertheless, what links "El costado" to those five poems is an emphasis on the body: a composite of plural relations and self-awareness, self-possession, linked to others' gaze and to the effects of their desires, trespasses, judgments on the body. For example, we read in "Paraguay IV": "Sacarse la suciedad del cuerpo / la sensacion de un abuso / de una muerte más grande // Sacarse / la muerte / con agua // El dolor dibuja una flor / y la mata" (2000). The floral metaphor, so prevalent in Machado's poems in *Marjal* and the wound, evident in all three of the women's works we have been discussing, center the relation of the voice to its re-appropriation of the body's painful experience, and a self-healing process. The autonomy is, thus, reclaimed through images of a physical vulnerability, an acceptance of the stain made by external vessels of death ("barcos" in "Paraguay I" or "el vendaval" in "El costado"), in the "they said" or "they gave" in Cerón's "América," and the "Hambre tensa: zarpazo" in Machado's poems.

On the other hand, the function of the body as separate from the voice, as the animal-pet of the self (as we've noted above is some of the poems), more openly in Machado and Colombino, signifies the breach between the pre- and post-nat(ion)al, the body exempted from that trajectory as the animal. The creaturely voice, un-subjected to the rule of law, except as complete or semi-exclusion (with conventional language the norm of utterability), reawakens as a *locus mobile, mobilias, agilitas* through space to recapture the focus of expression. Its location as an image on a screen, distanced from the real presence whose profound being it would seek to express, nonetheless finds plurality, alliance, in performing the poem; the world as audience now captured.

Sound Body and Collective Works

In contraposition to the above works that I have discussed by Lía Colombino, *Proyecto auricular* (2006) is a collective work by the Paraguayan poet with musician Javier Palma. It allows for greater expansión of the visual and musical interpretations of her texts. The CD of *Proyecto auricular* contains 12 tracks, 11 written by Colombino and one by Palma. The authors have called this work and "audioplaquette," which inaugurates the Ex Machina collection of Ediciones de la Ura whose purpose is to disseminate audiovisual material. The work was first presented in 2005 in various locations and in which Javier Palma performed the songs with his band *Los Detectives Salvajes*, and Lía Colombino as invited guest.

According to one review of the work, the record breaks with previous frameworks: "Los textos no son canciones, tampoco poemas. Son un lenguaje experimental en el que se conjugan textos literarios con música" (the texts are not songs, and they are not poems. They are an experimental language in which literary texts are melded with music) (ABC.com 2006). For the sound aspects of the compact disc's works, Palma utilized an array of electronic and acoustic musical instruments spanning vast cultural origins such as the guitar, the bass, the charango, the derbek (a drum originally played in Egypt, Armenia and Turkey), congas (from Cuba), and other instruments of percussion. The tracks also include the recorded sounds of quotidian objects, including those of clocks, cash registers, telephones, and hospital equipment.

In one such of the songs from *Proyecto auricular* titled "La última tarde," we see charactersitics similar to what we have examined in Melisa Machado's "El canto rojo," primarily the relevance of the female body to the expression of the relationship to a constricting space that is later subverted and transcended at once.

In this video containing Colombino's poem, the initial scene of the body focuses by the camera, in a darkened space, imply an ominous, imposing environment as well. The camera focus on the dancer's feet, then the contorting movements as she lifts herself from a brick-heavy set, finally stretches to the sky, echo the effort of the body to escape the weight of some burden. Interpreted and choreographed by Cinthia López, the video is 5:34 minutes in length, and feature an original musical score.

The first scene of "La última tarde" depits the hands and feet, first with an emphasis on the fingers of each hand, then on the toes and foot, against a tiled outer surface such as in a patio. The position of the dancer's body on the ground, with her face made visible only 2:25 minutes into the video, is animalistic in its pose, and suggestive of a menacing or disturbing atmosphere. The musical accompaniment is a minimalist arrangement of solo piano in a loose melody composed of dispersed and dissonant notes, in addition to the highpitched stringed sounds of the charango, a pre-Colombian Andean instrument of probably Quechua and Aymara origin that is said to belong to the lute family. Its arpeggios create a nuanced cloud of sound above the disconcerting and startling piano intercalations.

The dancer, dressed in a green, black, white and turquoise striped bathing suit and a hot pink headband, only arises from the floor with great effort. When she does, we see the sky behind her, and lush branches of trees. She seems disoriented and frightened. Finally, as she crawls and then lifts herself up, the music disappears, the light of day has turned dark. In an interior room, we hear a sound like a rushing wind and see the dancer against a black wall as she now moves in jerking motions to the beat of what sounds like a heart monitor. Different aspects of her face and hands are pictured as her image is filtered through various colour washes across the screen: green, red, purple, yellow and back to natural plane, also changing in time to the heart monitor beating rapidly [3:27–3:43]. The end of this portion takes the viewer into another dark scene now with the Green branches at night in the background The dancer moves in larger swaying motions.

When Colombino's words begin, the incessant sound of the heart monitor changes, first to a vacuous space, and then to a deep electronic bass that seems to descend the sound into an abyss. The camera focuces the dancer's torso. Colombino begins: "Es la hora que el cielo se pone color rosa y las nubes forman olas en el cielo. Es la útlima tarde del año. Las cigarras anuncian algo: la llegada del mes de enero. Su canto inunda la tarde que se convierte en noche. Sólo cuando callan, ella cae en la cuenta de aquel canto ininterrumpido" (It's the hour when the sky turns pink and the clouds form waves in the sky. It's the last afternoon of the year. The cicadas announce something: the arrival of the month of January. Their singing floods the afternoon that turns to night. Only when they sing, she notices that unending song). The sound track avoids the cliché of reproducing the sound of cicadas and instead maintains its steady progress almost out of time with the dancer. The foreboding is increased by the constant and unevenly spaced movement against the greenery framed by a black Wall and a harsh bright light upon her body.

As Colombino's verses continue, the repetition in the discursive format of the literary text is taken up by the echoes of her voice that superimpose words she speaks:

> Es la útlima tarde del año. Hay una calma pesada, hay cigarras, hay cielo color rosa, hay cigarras, algo se anuncia y ella, tirada en la cama con los ojos casi cerrados, ve venir lo que se aproxima con la calma de cientos de dromedarios en un desierto quieto, … de cientos de dromedarios en un desierto quieto,… de cientos de dromedarios en un desierto quieto…, en un desierto quieto…, en un desierto quieto…, en un desierto quieto…" [3:56–4:44].

> (It's the last afternoon of the year. There is a heavy calm, cicadas, a pink-coloured sky, cicadas, something anounces itself and, sprawled on her bed with her eyes almost closed, she sees something approach with the calm of hundreds of camels in a quiet desert, … of hundreds of camels in a quiet desert, … of hundreds of camels in a quiet desert…, in a quiet desert, … in a quiet desert,… in a quiet desert…)

Colombino's reading on the video is paced slowly in a neutral almost disaffected tone. Typical of contemporary poetry readings, here is none of the traditional impostation or declamative extroversión of more traditional poetry recital or of the greater theatrics of some spoken word performances. Here it is a monologue type meditation that interacts with the rest of the visual and sonoric elements in the generation of meaning.

The last scene of the video performance [4:45–5:34][15] strips all sound down to one percussive instrument, perhaps a clave, tapping quickly. Then, silence as the dancer lifts her arms to shoulder height and thrusts her head back as if in trance. The dream-like quality of the entire sequence of scenes leaves a trace of mystery, while the complex interjecting of sound, word and image beg deciphering.

---

[15] Recorded in Asunción in 2007, the version cited above is that which was uploaded by the authors to YouTube and made available on February 8, 2011.

MUSIC AND NOMADIC TIME

Memory plays a key role in pluralizing the sense of self, and this must be reconciled with the location of the subject vis-à-vis the body. If poetry is a metalanguage in constant movement—against the former stasis and towards a new, ever-expanding sense production—then for Colombino it is created by "rubbing together" words in the text in order to generate a spark of creation/combustion, whereby the past and present collide. This is achieved by the reaching from original oral production of the body and the earth, inspiration and sound, through its written word back into sound, image and rhythm; the oral-textual flows liberate the body through contact with the natural environment in an almost kinetic fusion of agency through green spaces. The body seen as the explorer of daily cycles releases the tension of the caged sub-terrain of the subject by sinking the "syllable" into an abyss. By contrast, in Machado poetry leans into the body's conscious awareness of its physicality, as an animalistic dance with the subject who is not always aware of how to decipher the body's communication. In Cerón, the ambiguously gendered protest against a colonial past, links and channels a personal affiliation with the past, as a working through the loss of her father, who takes over the voice of the poetic female subject in order to save it for something else. In Cerón's voice the fusion of the female and male voices (her father's death a catalyst into her living expression), her obsession with remaking the past as sound symbols in the present, points to a disintegration of a normative stance before language and the binary codes of gender.

For the occasion to represent their respective Latin American countries at the London 2012 Poetry Parnassus during the World Olympics, each of the three poets represented here selected specific texts that mirror anxious subjects who sense, in the affective relation to its body, ways out of the myriad reflections of the identities their incarnations are expected to portray. Machado's poem, "Jamba de flores negras," most clearly delineates the relation between the individual subject and its alliances with a large collective; this stance implies an alliance of hunger, even death ("pueblo de huesos"), which withstands the blows that we mentioned earlier. As we read in the first four strophes of her poem, adopting the initial instance of a verb in the "nosotros"/first person plural (we) form, as a "pueblo," the poetic voice urges all to "burn together with her"; as a grouping of bones, the action cedes subsequently to the chaos of rage ("radiante hueso") and deception ("toda lengua bífida").

The proclamations in the eighth verse, that whoever desires captivity will have it, restores agency even as it admits the dangerous tumult in which the subjects identify the animals. Yet it is precisely that animalistic sense of being that apparently possesses the power to liberate the subject. Despite the malice of the beast, fiercely manifesting a survival instinct (its thirst and hunger), the animalistic stance is nevertheless the agentic mode for attempting to absolve the subject of its "sin" or original wound/lack. Coming full circle to the "desgarro" in Machado's *Marjal* or wounding, that of "América" as witnessed in Cerón's text, and that of the struggling voice in Colombino's "El costado."

In his 2007 book *The Empire of Neomemory*, published in English translation in 2013 (translated by Jen Hofer, Christian Nager and Brian Whitener), Heriberto Yépez writes about the root of this wound as an American lesion, as well as a place of separation with the body's integrity. In his view, this represents "the American dream, the dream of expansionism in all its variants. It is with the purpose of understanding this empire that I have written this book. [Charles] Olson in and of himself does not interest me; I am interested in his character as a microanalogy for decoding the psychopoetics of Empire. Philosophy tries to comprehend reality through a discussion of abstract concepts produced by floating masculine heads (decapitalisms); in contrast, what I want to understand is the present via concrete bodies, historical microanalysis via the hunt for biosymbols. Using the text, I want to see through it to glimpse the *substructure* and the *superstructure*" (72-73). The three poems examined offer such glimpses, insofar as they attempt to uncover the interstices of self and collective across time and space in representational forms by writing through the body.

The body's plural symbolism must return to the body's grounded state. However, through its extensions, via cyberspaces and multiplied resonances in others, it can extend its reach. Whether it is totalizing in its simplified absorption of the other into its vision, or whether it can resist this and remain in a dynamic flow, is the caveat we glimpse in Yépez's counter-hegemonic proposition, and in the three poetic perspectives observed in Machado, Cerón and Colombino. Their resistance finds support in hypertext and video formats enfused with the lightning scope of the internet and its extensions. In his review of Yépez' *Empire of Neomemory*, Jerome Rothenberg has stated that "In this age of internet and blog, the possibility opens of a free circulation of works (poems and poetics in the present instance) outside of any commercial or academic nexus" (website). Rothenberg considers this "manner of a freewheeling on anthology or magazine… [to be] in the tradition of autonomous publication by poets, going back to Blake and Whitman and Dickinson, among numerous others" (website). Yépez's assertion that "writing is pantopic" implies its openness to "being or presenting a comprehensive or panoramic view" (his official website, 2015). As he presents this perspective against the backdrop of the tensions between "imperial time," on the one hand, and "nomadic plurality of time" (such as that of cyberspace) on the other, Yépez argues that the Empire attempts to suppress, contain and undo the latter.

The three women poets' works wrestle with this intersectional level of the body in time. An objective correlative in this awakened perception is the body as "mi animal," a distancing of the utter identification of self and embodiment, their poetic expression seeks release into a plurality of time viewed from a perspective that does not always coincide with the present. Still, the present time is the lens through which the various conscious positionings take place, and in which a continuum of moments is received in the aural and kinetic/rhythmic perceptions and sensations of the body as receptor, radar, vehicle and actor in the world, inherited or experienced directly.

REFERENCES

ABC Color. 2006. "'Proyecto auricular': una manera diferente de conjugar letra y música." Asunción, Paraguay. March 25, 2006. Accessed January 12, 2015. www.abc.com.py/espectaculos/proyecto-auricular-una-manera-diferente-de-conjugar-letra-y-musica-893673.html

Alemany, Eugenio, ed. 2012. *La borra del café* by Mario Benedetti. With notes and articles edited by Eugenio Alemany. Cordoba, Spain. Accessed: August 26, 2013. www.iesseneca.net/iesseneca/IMG/pdf/borra.pdf

Alcalá, Rosa, ed. 2012. *The Selected Performances of Cecilia Vicuña*. Edited and Translated by Rosa Alcalá New York: Ugly Duckling Presse.

Alcalá, Rosa and Vicuña, Cecilia. 2013. "The Poetics of Performance." A Conversation of Rosa Alcalá and Cecilia Vicuña on the Poetics of Performance. Recorded in New York on February 8th 2013 after the presentation of Spit Temple. Accessed October 24, 2013. http://vimeo.com/77621895.

Arredondo, Inés. 1991. "Canción de cuna." *Obras completas*. México, D.F.: Siglo XXI: 49–57.

———. 1980. *La señal* (short stories). México: Ediciones Era, 1965; 2nd ed.: México: UNAM.

———. 1986. *Río Subterráneo* (short stories). México: Joaquín Mortiz, 1979; 2nd ed.: México: Mortiz/SEP.

———. 1981. *La Sunamita y otros cuentos*. México: Secretaría de Educación Pública.

———. 1982. *Acercamiento a Jorge Cuesta* (Masters Thesis). México: SepSetentas Diana.

———. 1983. *Opus 123* (short stories). México: Editorial Oasis.

———. 1984. *Historia verdadera de una princesa* (short story for children). México: Reloj de Cuentos/CIDCLI/SEP.

———. n/y. Mariana. México: UNAM, Material de Lectura. Series: *El Cuento Contemporáneo* 2.

———. 1988. *Los Espejos* (short stories). México: Joaquín Mortiz.

———. 1988. *Obras completas*. México: Siglo XXI/DICOFUR Sinaloa.

Aronson, Alex. 1980. *Music and the Novel: A Study in Twentieth-Century Fiction*. Totowa, New Jersey: Rowman and Littlefield.

Atwood, Margaret. "The Poem/ The Song." *Art of Time Ensemble 2014/15 Concert Series Program*. Directed by Andrew Burashko. Toronto: Encave Theatre, Harbourfront Centre. November 7–8, 2014. 3.

Austin, J. L. 1962. *How to do things with words*. Cambridge: Harvard University Press.

Ayestarán, Lauro. 1969. *El folklore musical uruguayo*. Montevideo: Arca.

Baccino, Daniel. 2009-2012. "Music: Guitar, Winston Mombrú." *Sitio Personal de Daniel Baccino*. Punta del Diablo, Uruguay. December 2009 and July 2012. https://sites.google.com/site/personaldebacci/musica/guitarra/winston-mombru

Bachelard, Gaston. 1994. *The Poetics of Space* [*La Poétique de* l'Espace, 1958]. Translated by Maria Jolas. Boston: Beacon Press.

Barthes, Roland. 1985. *The Responsibility of Forms: Critical Essays on Music, Art, and Representation*. Translated by Richard Howard. Berkeley: University of California Press. 245–60.

———. 1975. *S/Z*. Translated by Richard Miller. London: Cape.

Benedetti, Mario. 1974. *Canciones de amor y desamor*. Collected in the 2003 recording with Favero.

———. 1972. *Canciones de la oficina*. Songs based on his poems from *Poemas de la oficina* (1953-1956).

———. 1983. *Canciones del desexilio*. Collected in the 2003 recording with Favero.

———. 1988. *Canciones del más acá*. México D.F., Nueva Imagen.

———. 2006. *Canciones del que no canta*. Buenos Aires: Seix Barral.

———. 1992. *Canciones nobles y sentimentales*. In the 2003 recording with Favero.
———. 1974. *Daniel Viglietti*. Gijón: Ediciones Júcar, Los Juglares.
———. 1992. *La borra del café*. Montevideo: Alfaguara.
———. 1973. *Letras de emergencia*. Buenos Aires: Editorial Alfa.
———. 1998. *Poemas de la oficina*. [1953-1956] Madrid: Visor.
———. 2001. *Preguntas al azar*. Madrid: Visor. [1986]
———. 1972. *Versos para cantar*. [See the 2003 recording with Favero.]
———. 1975. *Nacha Guevara canta a Benedetti*. Live at the Colegio de México:
    Presentation of *Canciones de la oficina*: "Sueldo," "Balada del empleado nuevo," "Amor de tarde," "Yo soy la secretaria," "Cuando te jubiles," "Guardería," "Aquí no hay cielo."
    Presentation, three *Versos para cantar*: "Vidalita, por las dudas," "De qué se ríe," "Vamos juntos." Presentation of three songs, *Canciones de amor y desamor*: "Todavía," "Vos lo dijiste (A la izquierda del roble)," "Te quiero." LP.
———. 1979. *Nacha Guevara en vivo*. With Benedetti y Favero. Live at the Teatro
    Hubert Le Blanc. Havana, Cuba. (reedited on CD in 1996) with the following tracks: Presentation (*Canciones de la oficina*), "Sueldo," "Balada del empleado nuevo," "Amor de tarde," "Dactilógrafo," "Cuando te jubiles," "Guardería," "Aquí no hay cielo." "Presentación (*Versos para cantar*), "Tu quebranto," "Vidalita, por las dudas," "Vamos juntos," "Oda a la pacificación," "Oda a la mordaza," "De qué se ríe;" "Presentación (*Canciones de amor y desamor*), "Te quiero," "A la izquierda del roble," "Todavía," "Hombre preso que besa a su hijo," "El triunfo de los muchachos," "Un padrenuestro latinoamericano." LP.
Benedetti, Mario and Alberto Favero. 2003. *Benedetti-Favero*. Singing by Adriana
    Varela, Jairo and Juan Carlos Baglietto. Acqua Records. CD.
Benedetti, Mario and Daniel Viglietti. 1985. *A dos voces*. Vol. I. Montevideo: Orfeo
    SCO 90749. Recording.
———. 1987. *A dos voces*. Vol. II. Montevideo: Orfeo SCO 90861. Recording.
———. 1994. *A dos voces* I and II. Montevideo: Orfeo CDO 047-2. Recording. Re-edition on compact disc of the first two albums.
———. 1994. *A dos voces*. Madrid: Visor. Book.
Beverley, John, Michael Aronna and José Oviedo. 1995. *The Postmodernism Debate
    in Latin America*. Durham: Duke University Press.
Bhabha, Homi K. 2006. "Cultural Diversity and Cultural Differences." *The Post-
    Colonial Studies Reader*, ed. B. Ashcroft, G. Griffiths, H. Tiffin. New York: Routledge. http://monumenttotransformation.org/atlas-of-transformation/html/c/cultural-diversity/cultural-diversity-and-cultural-differences-homi-k-bhabha.html
———. 1990. *Nation and Narration*. New York: Routledge.
———. 2002. "On Cultural Respect." *Multiculturalism in Contemporary
    Societies: Perspectives on Difference and Transdifference*. Ed. Helmbrecht Breinig, Jürgen Gebhardt, and Klauss Lösch. Erlangen: Universitätsverbund Erlangen-Nürnberg. 53–67.
———. 2004. *The Location of Culture*. New York: Routledge.
Bloodsworth-Lugo, Mary K. 2007. *Sexual Difference, Race, and Sexuality*. New
    York: State University of New York Press.
Borderlands: The Crossroads of Science and Spirit. September 13, 2011.
    http://borderlandresearch.com/book/metal-power/copper-the-substance-of-venus
Bouffartique, Rafael Oscar M. 1953. Lyrics to "Burundanga." EMI Music
    Publishing; renewed 1951 by Morro Music Corp. EMI Catalogue Partnership.
Bradu, Fabienne. 1987. *Señas particulares, escritora: ensayos sobre escritoras mexicanas del siglo XX*.
    México: Fondo de Cultura Económica.
Brito, Eugenia, ed. 1998. *Antología de poetas chilenas. Confiscación y silencio*. Santiago de Chile: Dolmen Ediciones.

References

Butler, Judith. 2011. "Bodies in Alliance and the Politics of the Street." *Transversal – eipcp webjournal.* [europäisches institute für progressive kulturpolitik] *Eipcp.net* (Sept.): n. pag. Accessed July 3, 2014.www.eipcp.net/transversal/1011/butler/en.

———. 1993. *Bodies That Matter: On the Discursive Limits of "Sex."* New York: Routledge.

———. 1994. "Gender as Performance: An Interview with Judith Butler," *Radical Philosophy: A Journal of Socialist and Feminist Philosophy* 67 (Summer): 32–39. www.theory.org.uk/but-int1.htm

———. 1999. *Gender Trouble: feminism and the subversion of identity*. New York: Routledge.

———. 2005. *Giving an Account of Oneself*. New York: Fordham University Press.

———. 1990. "Performative Acts and Gender Constitution: An Essay in Phenomenology and Feminist Theory." *Performing Feminisms: Feminist Critical Theory and Theatre*. Ed. Sue-Ellen Case. Baltimore: Johns Hopkins Uinversity Press.

Butler, Judith and Athena Athanasiou. 2014. *Dispossession: The Performative in the Political*. 2013. Malden, MA: Polity.

Butler, Judith and Gayatri Chakravorty Spivak. 2007. *Who Sings the Nation-State? Language, Politics, Belonging*. New York: Seagull Books.

Cabel, Andrea. 2011. "El performance: '¿Una esponja mutante y nómada?'". *Porta 9: disección literaria*. 8 October. Accessed October 13, 2011. www.porta9.com/?p=129

Canon U.S.A. 1999. *Mobile Marketing Vehicle Glides to U.S. Hot Air Balloon National Championships*.

Cerón, Rocío. 2005. *Apuntes para sobrevivir al aire*. Mexico: Ediciones Urania.

———. 2002. *Basalto*. Mexico, D.F.: Ediciones Sin Nombre.

———. 2013. "Borealis, Rocío Cerón y Chefa Alonso: Poesía e improvisaciones sonoras," Spoken Word. Institute of Mexico in Spain, *YouTube*, Madrid 2013. www.youtu.be/v_HRaUwRRqo.

———. 2012. *Diorama*. Mexico UANL-Tabasco.

———. 2013. *Diorama*. (Bilingual edition: Spanish/English) Translated byAnna Rosen Guerco. New York: Diaz Grey Editores.

———. 2013. *Diorama*. Madrid: Amargord Ediciones, Serie Candela.

———. 2014. *Diorama*. (Bilingual edition: Spanish/English) Translated by Anna Rosenwong. Los Angeles: Phoneme Media.

———. 2011. "Diorama by Rocío Cerón & Nómada." Videopoem (Spanish and English). Mexico, 2011. *YouTube*. Uploaded January 11, 2012. Accessed May 7, 2015. www.youtu.be/bUnl3cff8KQ

———. 2009. "Imperio." Book/CD/Video/Interdisciplinary Action. Motín Poeta / Imperio. DR: México, D.F.

———. 2008. *Imperio*. Mexico: Ediciones Monte Caramelo.

———. 2001. *Litoral*. Guadalajara: Filodecaballos.

———. 2012. Reading of the poem "América" in a video titled "Rocío Ceron – Mexico." Poetry Parnassus by Southbank Centre. July 26. YouTube. Accessed April 25, 2014. www.youtube.com/watch?v=P4Z5d1Ntwl4

———. 2009. Rocío Cerón: Official Website. Accessed May 5, 2013. www.rocioceron.com/bajar_libros.html

———. 2003. *Soma*. Buenos Aires: Eloísa Ediciones.

———. 2010. *Tiento*. Mexico: Universidad Autónoma de Nuevo León.

———. 2012. *Tiento*. (German edition) Translated by Simone Reinhard. Berlin: Hans Shiller.

———. 2012. *Tiento* (Swedish edition) Translated by Ulrika Serling. Malmö, Sweden:

Aura Latina.
Cerón, Rocío and Bishop, Nómada, Tower, Pizarro. 2009. *Imperio/Empire* (interdisciplinary bilingual edition). Mexico: CONACULTA-FONCA.
Chambers, Samuel A. and Terrell Carver. 2008. *Judith Butler and Political Theory: Troubling Politics*. New York: Routledge.
Chávez, Benjamín. 2003. "POESÍA ES +." [Interview of Nadia Prado and Malú Urriola] Pulso. Suplemento literario: *"Salamandra."* (La Paz-Bolivia). Accessed February 22, 2012. www.letras.s5.com/poesiaesmas1.htm
Clark, Meredith. 2012. "Master Weaver: The Mother Tongue and the Genesis of Language in 'I TU' by Cecilia Vicuña." *XXII Congress of the Asociación Internacional de Literatura y Cultura Femenina Hispánica* (AILFCH). "De la tierra al ciberespacio / Between the Earth and Cyberspace." Grand Valley State University. Grand Rapids, Michigan. November 10.
Colombino, Lía. 2000. *Cavidades ausentes*. Asunción: Cuadernos de la Ura/Editorial Arandura.
———. 2011. "La última tarde (videodanza) / Javier Valdez." *YouTube*. February 8, 2011. Accessed January 11, 2012. www.youtu.be/DsyYnXU4560 ———.
2009. *Lupa*. Asunción: Ediciones de la Ura.
———. 2012. "Paraguay en cinco poemas." (from her book *Tierra de secano*), Spoken Word Festival Escalinata Abierta. *YouTube*. 14 May 2012, Accessed May 7, 2015. www.youtu.be/LRFDymmDz34.
———. 2006. *Proyecto Auricular*. Asunción: Ediciones de la Ura, Asunción: Ediciones de la Ura. Audio-plaquette.
———. 2012. Reading of the poem "El costado" in a video titled "Lia [sic] Colombino – Paraguay." Poetry Parnassus, Southbank Centre. July 25, 2012. YouTube. Accessed April 25, 2014. www.youtube.com/watch?v=wrRQR7hUmHA&index=44&list=PLC5046D46F1754A38
———. 2001. *Tierra de secano*. Asunción: Ediciones de la Ura.
Correa-Díaz, Luis and Scott Weintraub, eds. 2016. *Poetry and Digital Poetics*. Buenos Aires: Editorial Universidad Central.
———, 2010/2011. "Introducción: Literatura latinoamericana, española, portuguesa en la era digital (nuevas tecnologías y lo literario)" [Introduction: Latin American, Spanish and Portuguese Literature in the Digital Era (New Technologies and the Literary)]. Special Edition: "Nuevas tecnologías y lo literario." *Arizona Journal of Hispanic Cultural Studies* 14 (2010/2011): 147-365.
———. 2006. Poesía y poéticas digitales / electrónicas / tecnos / new-media en América *Latina*. Edited by Luis Correa-Díaz and Scott Weintraub. Buenos Aires: Universidad Central. Accessed June 30, 2014. www.goo.gl/rILOFz
Cortázar, Julio. 2001. "El interrogador." *Salvo el crepúsculo*. 1984. Buenos Aires: Alfaguara.
———. 1995. *El perseguidor*. Buenos Aires: Alianza Cien. [1959]
———. 1959. *Las armas secretas*. Buenos Aires: Editorial Sudamericana.
———. 2010. *Rayuela*. Madrid: Punto de Lectura. [1963]
———. 1984. *Salvo el crepúsculo*. Mexico, D.F.: Nueva Imagen.
———. 2016. *Save twilight:* Selected poems of Julio Cortázar. [*Salvo el crepúsculo*, 1984] Translated by Stephen Kessler. San Francisco: City Lights Books.
Coulson, Joseph. 2007. *Of Song and Water*. New York: Archipelago Books.
"Creating Worlds." *Transversal – eipcp webjournal*. [europäisches institute für progressive kulturpolitik] *Eipcp.net* Sept (2011): n. pag. Accessed July 18, 2014. http://eipcp.net/projects/creatingworlds/files/about/

References

Curl, John. 2003. "The Flower Songs of Nezahualcoyotl. Ancient Nahua (Aztec) Poetry." Excerpts from *Ancient American Poets*, translated from Nahuatl, Maya and Quechua, and compiled, by John Curl. *Bilingual Review / La Revista Bilingüe* 26: 2/3, Ancient American Poets (MAY-DECEMBER 2001-2002), pp. iii–v, vii–ix, 1, 3–13, 15–43, 45–55, 57–101, 103–107, 109, 111–123, 125–147, 149–155, 157–163. Full text available at: www.jstor.org/stable/25745755. Accessed February 23, 2017.
www.famsi.org/research/curl/nezahualcoyotl_intro.html
Digital Latin American Cultures Network. "Researching the Cultural Dimensions of New Media in Latin America. DLAC Network, Events, News, 22 Apr. 2013, latamcyber.wordpress.com/2013/04/22/report-on-literaturas-plurales/.
Eliade, Micea. 1963. "The Moon & its Mystique." *Patterns in Comparative Religion*. New York: Meridian Book, The World Publishing Company. 180.
Eskelinen, Markku. *Cybertext Poetics: The Critical Landscape of New Media Literary Theory*. Bloomsbury Publishing, 2012.
Esquivel, Laura. 2001. *Between Two Fires: Intimate Writings on Life, Love, Food and Flavor*. Translated by Steven Lytle. New York: Crown Publishers. (First published in 1995 *Íntimas suculencias: Tratado Filosófico de Cocina*.)
———. 1989. *Como agua para chocolate*. Mexico, D.F.: Planeta.
———. 2002. *El libro de las emociones: Son de la razón sin corazón*. Barcelona: Plaza y Janés Editores. (Non-fiction)
———. 2013. *Escribiendo la nueva historia o cómo dejar de ser víctima en doce lecciones*. Mexico, D.F.: Suma de Letras.
———. 1998. *Íntimas suculencias: Tratado Filosófico de Cocina*. Madrid: Ollero & Ramos.
———. 1995. *La ley del amor*. Buenos Aires: Grijalbo.
———. 1996. *La ley del amor*. New York: Random House.
———. 2000. *La ley del amor*. Bogotá: Plaza y Janés.
———. 2004. *La ley del amor*. New York: Random House.
———. 2009. *La ley del amor*. Bogotá: Plaza y Janés.
———. 2015. *La ley del amor*. Santiago, Chile: Delbolsillo.
———. 1992. *Like Water for Chocolate*. Translated by Thomas Christensen and Carol Christensen. Toronto: Double Day.
———. 1994. *Like Water for Chocolate*. Translated by Thomas Christensen and Carol Christensen. New York: Anchor Books.
———. 2006. *Malinche*. Mexico, D.F.: Alfaguara/Santillana.
———. 2006. *Malinche*. Translated by Ernesto Mestre-Reed. New York: Atria Books.
———. Interview. "Necesitamos romper con la ide de que nada nos vincula al otro: Laura Esquivel." May 3, 2013. "Cultura." *La Jornada*. Accessed May 10, 2013. www.jornada.unam.mx/2013/05/03/cultural=/a05n1cul
———. 2001. *Swift as Desire*. Translated by Stephen Lytle. New York: Crown Publishers. (First published in 2001 in Spanish as *Tan veloz como el deseo*).
———. 2002. *Swift as Desire*. Translated by Stephen Lytle. New York: Anchor Books, 2002.
———. 2001. *Tan veloz como el deseo*. Barcelona: Plaza y Janés Editores.
———. 1996. *The Law of Love*. Translated by Margaret Sayers Peden. New York: Crown Publishing.
———. 1997. *The Law of Love*. Toronto: Three Rivers Press, Penguin Canada.
———. 2014. Interview. "Writing the Future." http://sanmiguelwritersconference2014.org/ February 14, 2014. Accessed February 21, 2014.
Felipe, Liliana. 1995. Lyrics from "Mala," "Nadie," "San Miguel Arcángel," and "A Su Merced." *Liliana Felipe*. Mexico, D.F.: Ediciones el Hábito. *La ley del amor*. Buenos Aires: Grijalbo: 61, 98, 165, 200, 233. (The sound recordings of these songs appear on the accompanying CD as tracks 2, 3, 6, 8 and 10 *respectively).*

Felluga, Dino. 2011. "Modules on Butler: On Performativity." *Introductory Guide to Critical Theory*. January 31. Purdue U. Accessed October 13, 2011.

Fernández-Levin, Rosa. 1997. "Bridging the Gap: Mythical and Historical Discourse in *La ley del amor*." *Journal of Latin American Lore* 20 (2): 333-346.

Figueredo, Maria L. 2014. "Embodied Texts and Musical Readings: The Multimedia Novel by Laura Esquivel." *International Guest Lecture: Maria Figueredo*. School of International Letters and Cultures. Arizona State University. Tempe, Arizona. January 23, 2014.

———. "Embodied Texts and Musical Readings: The Multimedia Novel by Laura Esquivel." XXI Annual Congress of the AILCFH: "Habitar el género / Inhabiting Gender." Universitat de Barcelona, Spain. Conference session: "En diálogo: género, literatura y otras artes [In Dialogue: Gender, Literature and Other Arts], October 19-21, 2011.

———. 2001/2002. "El eterno retorno entre la poesía y la música popular" ['Eternal Recurrence' in Poetry and Popular Music]. *Revista Canadiense de Estudios Hispánicos (RCEH)* XXVI (1-2): 299-319.

———. 1999. "Entre la poesía oral y la escrita: la canción y la cultura literaria" [Between Oral and Written Poetry: The Song and Literary Culture]. "La inscripción de la oralidad en las culturas latinoamericanas" [The Inscription of Orality in Latin American Cultures]. *Estudios hispánicos en la red*. 10 Sept. 1999.

———. 2015. "Gaming Poetry in Wor(l)d Play: Poetry and Video Games in Latin American Poetic Practice." Invited Speaker. Transatlantic Graduate Studies Seminar, University of Western Ontario, 6 Nov. 2015.

———. 2003. "Latin American Song as an Alternative Voice in the New World Order." In Gordana Yovanovich, ed., *The New World Order: Corporate Agenda and Parallel Reality*. Montreal: McGill-Queen's University Press. 178-200.

———. 2016. "Networked Poetries: Two Latin American Perspectives." *The International Journal of Communication and Media Studies (inaugural volume): New Media, Technology, and the Arts* 1 (1): 23-29. www.ijp.cgpublisher.com/product/pub.336/prod.6

———. 2005. Poesía y canto popular: Su convergencia en el siglo XX. Uruguay, 1960-*1985*. (*Poetry and Popular Song: Their Convergence in the Twentieth Century. The Case of Uruguay, 1960-1985.*) Montevideo: Linardi y Risso.

———. 2011. "Trayectoria y proyección del enunciado femenino, o la revolución en poesía musicalizada, del Canto Popular Uruguayo: El caso del dúo Cristina Fernández y Washington Carrasco en 'Canto de madre'". ["Mother's Song: Feminine Revolt Surfacing in the *Canto Popular Song* of the Duo Washington Carrasco and Cristina Fernández]. Colombia. *Cuadernos de música, artes visuales y artes escénicas* 6: 1 (Jan-March): 53-64. www.cuadernosmusicayartes.javeriana.edu.co/

Gallo, Paola. Interview by Leopoldo de Quevedo at the Primer Encuentro Internacional de Mujeres poetas en el País de las Nubes en el Camino del Café.Oaxaca, Mexico. "La poeta uruguaya PAOLA GALLO habla del erotismo en la poesía de tres poetisas de su país." [5:45] YouTube. Accessed September 10, 2012. Video.

Gambetti, Zeynep. 2014. Rev. of *Dispossession: The Performative in the Political* by Judith Butler and Athena Athanasiou. *Signs* 40 (1): 255–258.

Gelman, Juan. 1962. *Gotán*. Buenos Aires: Ediciones Horizonte.

Goodchild, Veronica. 2012. *Songlines of the Soul: Pathways to a New Vision for a New Century*. Lake Worth, Florida: Nicolas-Hays.

Guevara, Nacha. 1996. *Nacha canta Benedetti*. Live with Benedetti and Favero at the Teatro Hubert De Blanc in Havana, Cuba, with the RTV Symphonic Orchestra of Spain. Directed by Favero. Re-edited for CD.

References

Hagenbüchle, Roland. 2008. "Transcending Hybridity – Recovering Difference." *Hybrid Americas: Contacts, Contrasts, and Confluences in New World Literatures and Cultures*. Eds. Josef Raab and Martin Butler. Tempe, Arizona: Lit Bilingual Press/ Editorial Bilingüe. 379–89.

Haupt, Jennifer. 2014. "Jane Hirshfield: Why Write Poetry? Poetry is a release of something previously unknown into the visible." Column: "One True Thing." *Psychology Today*. January 6. Accessed January 17, 2014. www.psychologytoday.com/blog/one-true-thing/201401/jane-hirshfield-why-write-poetry.

Hawking, Stephen and Leonard Mlodinow. 2012. *The Grand Design*. New York: Bantam.

Hellauer, Brian. 1993. *Up, Up and Away. Boatmen's Bancshares Inc. Buys Hot-Air Balloon for Marketing Purposes* 158. Web. September 21, 2012.

Huidobro, Vicente. 1931. *Altazor*. Buenos Aires: Compañía Iberoamericana.

———. 1919. *Manifiesto Creacionista*. París.

Hunt, Valerie. 1996. *Quantum Physics: Infinite Mind*. Malibu, California: Malibu Publishing Company.

Irigaray, Luce. 2002. *To Speak is Never Neutral*. 1985. Translated by Gail Schwab. New York: Routledge.

———. 2002. *Between East and West: From Singularity to Community*. 1999. Translated by Stephen Pluháček. New York: Columbia University Press.

Kaiser, Kevin. 2014. "Rewriting the Rules of Marketing." *Writers' Yearbook 2014*. (Winter): 35–38. WritersDigest.com. Web. January 21, 2015.

Kristeva, Julia. 1999. *El porvenir de la revuelta*. [*L'avenir d'une revolte*, 1998, Calmann-Lévy] Buenos Aires: Fondo de la Cultura Económica de Argentina.

———. 2002. *Revolt, She Said*. Sylvere Lotringer, ed. Translated by Brian O'Keefe. Nueva York: Semitotext(e).

———. 1984. *Revolution in Poetic Language*. [*La révolution du langage poétique*, 1974]. New York: Columbia University Press.

———. 1980. Séméiotiké: Recherches pour une sémanalyse. Paris: Seuil.

———. 1975. "The system and the speaking subject." In Sebeok, Thomas A. (ed.), *The Tell Tale Sign. A Survey of Semiotics. Lisse*, Netherlands: The Peter de Ridder Press. 47–55.

Las Últimas Noticias. 1998. "Poesía de Malú Urriola y Nadia Prado: La rebeldía frente al desencanto." Tuesday, December 22. *Proyecto Patrimonio: El salón de lectura en español de internet*. Accessed June 15, 2012. www.letras.s5.com

Landow, George P. 2006. *Hypertext 3.0: Critical Theory and New Media in an Era of Globalization*. Baltimore, Maryland: John Hopkins University Press.

László, Ervin. 2008. *The Quantum Shift in the Global Brain: How the New Scientific Reality Can Change Us and Our World*. Rochester, Vermont: Inner Traditions.

León-Portilla, Miguel. 1978. *Trece Poetas del Mundo Azteca*. Secretaría de Educación Pública. Universidad Nacional Autónoma de México. Also published online in PFD Format: September 2, 2016. Available at: www.historicas.unam.mx/publicaciones/publicadigital/libros/trece_poetas/mundo_azteca.html

Lyotard, Jean-Francois. 1984. *The Postmodern Condition: A Report on Knowledge*. Manchester: Manchester University Press.

Machado, Melisa. 2000. *Adarga*. (unpublished: collected in *Rituales*, 2011)

———. 2013. "Canto Rojo." *YouTube*. Visual effects by Cristóbal Severín Garcés. Music by Pablo Bonilla (DJ, producer and remixer: Boni). Centro Cultural de España, Montevideo. November 11, 2013. Uploaded May 23, 2013 to *YouTube*. Accessed August 20, 2015. www.youtu.be/R8YX4LRr2bI.

———. 2015. *El canto rojo*. Montevideo: Sediento Ediciones.

———. 2013. "El Canto Rojo de Melisa Machado." [The Red Song by Melisa Machado] Video. Presentation of *El Canto Rojo* at the Centro Cultural de España, Montevideo. Poetry and

performance by Melisa Machado. Visual effects by Cristóbal Severín Garcés. Music by Boni. May 2013. *Vimeo*. Accessed August 23, 2015. www.vimeo.com/74843531.
———. 2005. *El lodo de la estirpe*. Montevideo: Editorial Artefato.
———. 2007/2008. *Flores Negras*. (unpublished)
———. 2006. *Jamba de Flores Negras*. (unpublished, collected in *Rituales*, 2011)
———. 2008. *Marjal*. (unpublished: collected in *Rituales*, 2011)
———. 2012. "Melisa Machado." Blog. July 29, 2012, melisamachado.blogspot.ca/.
———. 2016. "Melisa Machado." Montevideo. Video. Project selected by the Fondo Concursable para la Cultura, Ministerio de Educación y Cultura, Dirección Nacional de Cultura, Uruguay. September 2016. *Vimeo*. Accessed November 2, 2016. www.vimeo.com/181689061
———. 2016. "Melisa Machado, 3 poemas 3 (+1)." May 13, 2016. Video. Accessed November 2, 2016. www. emmagunst.blogspot.ca/2016/05/melisa-machado-3-poemas-3-1.html.
———. 2008. Melisa Machado et al. Video of Live Performance. "Encuentro de poesía experimental: Colectivo JAM." Performance "Uno – Jam" por Colectivo JAM (Javier Bassi, Andrea Carvallo, Melisa Machado y Laura Moreno). 2008. Accessed November 2, 2016. www.vimeo.com/3886939
———. 2012. Reading of "Marjal" in a video titled "Melisa Machado, Uruguay." Poetry Parnassus, Southbank Centre. July 12. YouTube. Accessed April 25, 2014. www.youtube.com/watch?v=50jludtLNcI&list=PLC5046D46F1754A38&index=86
———. 1994. *Ritual de las Primicias*. Montevideo: Editorial Imaginarias.
———. 2011. *Rituales*. Montevideo: Editorial Estuario.
Magroni, Maria. 2005. "The Lost Foundation: Kristeva's Semiotic Chora and Its Ambiguous Legacy." *Hypatia* 20:1 (Winter): 78-98.
Maldonado de Oliveira, Debora. 2011. "Teaching Strategies in the Classroom: Laura Esquivel's Multimedia Novel *The Law of Love*." Literature and the Other Arts Session. Friday, October 7. 65th Annual Rocky Mountain Modern Language Association (RMMLA) Convention. Scottsdale, Arizona.
Menely, Tobias. 2015. *The Animal Claim: Sensibility and the Creaturely Voice*. Chicago: University of Chicago Press.
Mesa, Paula and Sergio Balderrabano. "Los elementos constitutivos del tango de la Guardia Vieja en Relación a los aportes realizados por músicos de formación académica." *SEDICI: Repositorio Institucional de la UNLP*. 2006. II Jornadas de Investigación en Disciplinas Artísticas y Proyectuales (La Plata, Argentina, 2006). PDF. Accessed January 11, 2016. http://sedici.unlp.edu.ar/bitstream/handle/10915/39169/Documento_completo.pdf?sequence=1
Mitidieri, María Carmela. 1997. "Los versos se hacen canciones." In *Mario Benedetti: Inventario Cómplice* by Carmen Alemany, Remedios Mataix and José Carlos Rovira. Alicante. *Biblioteca Virtual Miguel de Cervantes*. www.cervantesvirtual.com/obra-visor/mario-benedetti-inventario-complice--0/html/ff1470c0-82b1-11df-acc7-002185ce6064_93.html
Moi, Toril. 1985. "Marginality and subversion: Julia Kristeva*.*" *Sexual Textual Politics: Feminist Literary Theory*. New York: Routledge.
Moore Willingham, Elizabeth. 2010. *Laura Esquivel's Mexican Fictions: Like Water for Chocolate, The Law of Love, Swift as Desire, Malinche: A Novel*. Thornhill, Canada: Sussex Academic Press.
Mora, Gladys E. 2000. "La hibridación en la novela, tendencia o género al fin del milenio." *Revista de la Facultad de Filosfía y Humanidades, Universidad de Chile* 13 (Summer). http://web.uchile.cl/publicaciones/cyber/13/tx16.html
Munro, Don. 1985. "In New Age of Marketing, the Meter is the Message (Banks)." November 8. American Banker 150. Accessed September 21, 2012.

References

Nachón, Andi. 2000. "Nadia Prado: Sinceridad sin gentilezas." *Letras.s5.com: Página chilena al servicio de la cultura. Proyecto Patrimonio: Escritores y Poetas en Español*. Luis Martínez Solorza. Accessed May 6, 2010.
www.letras.s5.com/nadia1.htm

Nagam, Julie. 2016. "New Ground." *Canadian Art* (Winter 2016): 90-93.

Nattiez, Jean-Jacques. 1990. "Musical Meaning: The Symbolic Web." *In Music and Discourse: Toward a Semiology of Music*. Translated by Carloyn Abbate. Princeton, New Jersey: Princeton University Press.

Nehru, Meesha. 2004."A Future Mexican National Identity?: Laura Esquivel's LA LEY DEL AMOR." *Latinoamérica* 38: 217-232.

Nelson, A. A. 2007. "(Re)Inscribing Memory within the Chilean Post-Dictatorship Landscape: Recent Art Actions by Malú Urriola and Nadia Prado." *Journal of Latin American Cultural Studies* 16 (2): 201-217.

Nezahualcóyotl. "Percibo lo secreto…" ("I sense the secret, the dark truth…"). In
Zurita, Raul, ed. 2014. *Pinholes in the Night: Selected Poems from Latin America*. Translated by Forrest Gander. Port Townsend, Washington: Copper Canyon Press. N.p.

Newman, Eric. 2008. Honda Gets a Lift at Balloon Fest. (The Ex Files: The Latest and Greatest in Experiential Marketing). 49.

"No." 2012. Dir. Pablo Larraín. Perf. Gael García Bernal. Based on the unpublished play "El Plebiscito" by Antonio Skármeta. Sony. Film.

Paoletti, Mario. 1995. *El aguafiestas. La biografía de Mario Benedetti*. Buenos Aires:
Seix Barral.

"Particle Fever: With One Switch Everything Changes" [documentary]. 2013. Dir. Mark A. Levinson. Anthos Media. Film.

Pereira, Marcelo. 2016. "Era hora." *La Diaria*. Montevideo, Uruguay. October 14,
2016. https://ladiaria.com.uy/articulo/2016/10/era-hora/

Pequeño Glazier, Loss. 2001. *Digital poetics: the making of e-poetries*. University of
Alabama Press.

Picoult, Jodi. 2011. *Sing you Home*. Toronto: Atria Books, Simon & Shuster. Book
and CD.

Pfeiffer, Erna. 1992. "Hablar de literatura y no hablar de mí." *EntreVistas: Diez
escritoras mexicanas desde Bastidores*. Vervuert: Frankfurt am Main. 11–24.

Poniatowska, Elena. 2014. "We can all be writers." Distinguished Visiting Writer: Elena Poniatowska. September 18, 2014. Arizona State University. Tempe, US. Lecture.

Prado, Nadia. 1998. *Carnal*. Santiago: Cuarto Propio.

———. 2003. *©Copyright*. Buenos Aires: Editores Independientes.

———. 1992. *Simples placeres*. Santiago: Cuarto propio.

Prado, Nadia, and Malú Urriola. 2002. *POESÍA ES* +. Intervención urbana y lectura de poesía en globos de aire. [Urban Intervention with Poetry Reading in Hot Air Balloons] With photographs by Brown José y Magdalena Guevara, and Claudia Nelson. Santiago, Chile.

Prado, Miguelanxo. 1995. Illustrations/Comic grids. *La ley del amor*. Buenos Aires: Grijalbo. Pp. 52–59; 123–130; 143–150; 187–194; 216–223; 244–251.

Prieto, Antonio Stambaugh. 2002. "En torno a los estudios del *performance*, la teatralidad, y más" (notas para una conferencia). 1995. *Performancelogía: Todo sobre Arte de Performance y Performancistas*. Centro Regional de Investigaciones Multidisciplinarias, UNAM. September 13, 2002. http://performancelogia.blogspot.ca/2007/08/en-torno-los-estudios-del-performance.html

Protevi, John. 2001. *Political Physics: Deleuze, Derrida and the Body Politic*. London and New York: The Athlone Press.

Proyecto Patrimonio: El salón de lectura en español de internet. 2000. "Intervención Poética Aérea: Los versos caen del cielo." Accessed June 15, 2012. www.letras.s5.com

———. 1998. "Poesía de Malú Urriola y Nadia Prado: La rebeldía frente al desencanto." *Las últimas noticia*s. December 22.

Puig, Manuel. 1976. *El beso de la mujer araña*. Barcelona: Seix Barral.

———. 1979. *Kiss of the Spider Woman*. Translated by Thomas Colchie. New York: Alfred A. Knopf.

———. 1985. *Kiss of the Spider Woman*. Embrafilme/Island Alive/FilmDallas Pictures (US). Film.

Ralston Saul, John. *On Equilibrium*. Toronto, Penguin Canada, 2002.

Ricoeur, Paul. 1981. *Hermeneutics and the Human Sciences*: Essays on Language, Action and Interpretation. Edited and translated by John B. Thompson. London: Cambridge University Press.

———. 2007. *From Text to Action*. 1986. Translated by Kathleen Blamey and John B. Thompson. Evanston, Ill.: Northwestern University Press.

———. 2000. *The Just*. 1995. Translated by David Pellauer. Chicago: University of Chicago Press.

———. 2004. *Memory, History, Forgetting. 2000*. Translated by Kathleen Blamey and David Pellauer. Chicago: University of Chicago Press.

———. 2007. *Reflections on the Just*. 2001. Translated by David Pellauer. Chicago: University of Chicago Press.

———. 2004. *The Rule of Metaphor*. 1975. Translated by Robert Czerny. 4th ed. Routledge, Toronto. [The first edition in English was published by the University of Toronto Press, 1977. This English translation was rendered from the original manuscript, "La métaphore vive" and in consultation with Ricoeur, not from the first French published edition of the work in 1975 by Éditions de Seuil, Paris, as several errors were found by Ricoeur in the first print edition.]

Rodríguez Saavedra, Sergio and Bernardo Chandía Fica. 2000. "Intimidad Urbana: Huellas de los Últimos Poetas del Siglo Veinte." *Portal de Revistas Académicas de La Universidad de Chile* 14 (Fall). 8 pages (in PDF format). Web July 24, 2014. www.revistas.uchile.cl/index.php/RCH/article/view/9096.

Rothenberg, Jerome. 2013. Blog: Poems and Poetics. "Heriberto Yépez: From 'The Empire of Neomemory'." May 5. Accessed September 19, 2014. https://jacket2.org/commentary/heriberto-y%C3%A9pez-empire-neomemory

Rushdie, Salmon. *Imaginary Homelands: Essays and Criticism*, 1981–1991. New York: Penguin, 1992.

Salih, Sara. 2007. "On Judith Butler and Performativity." *Sexualities and Communication in Everyday Life: A Reader*. Eds. Karen E. Lovas and Mercilee M. Jenkins. Thousand Oaks, California: Sage. 55-68.
http://faculty.georgetown.edu/irvinem/theory/Salih-Butler-Performativity-Chapter_3.pdf

Sánchez, Luis Rafael. 1988. *La importancia de llamarse Daniel Santos*. Ediciones del Norte: Hanover.

Sánchez, Enriquillo. 1993. *Musiquito: Anales de un déspota y de un bolerista*. Madison, The University of Wisconsin: Taller.

Schild, Verónica. 2003. *Democracy in Latin America 30 Years after Chile's 9/11 Conference*. SUNY-Albany. Albany, New York. October 10-12. Remarks at the plenary session.

Sellers, Julie A. 2004. *Merengue and Dominican Identity: Music as National Unifier*. McFarland.

———. 2014. *Bachata and Dominican Identity / La bachata y la identidad dominicana*. Foreword by Darío Tejeda. Jefferson, North Carolina: McFarland.

Serrat, Joan Manuel and Mario Benedetti. 1985. *El sur también existe*. Ariola. LP.

Shapero, Rich. 2010. *Too Far*. Los Angeles: Outside Reading. Book and CD. [The CD is titled *Dawn Remembers*.]

Simanowksi, Roberto. "Digital Anthropophagy: Refashioning Words as Image, Sound and Action." *Leonardo* 43 (2): 159-163.

———. 2016. *Digital humanities and digital media conversations on politics, culture, aesthetics, and literacy*. London, England: Open Humanities Press.

References

Southbank Centre website. 2012. Poetry Parnassus. July–September 2012. Video Series. Accessed May 2, 2015. www.youtube.com/playlist?list=PLC5046D46F1754A38

Stewart, Ri and Renee Slade, Dir. 2009. "The Quantum Activist." Performed by Amit Goswami. Bluedot Productions. Film. Web. May 15, 2013. www.quantumactivist.com/

Taylor, Claire Louise. 2002. "Body-Swapping and Genre-Crossing: Laura Esquivel's 'La ley del amor'." *The Modern Language Review* 97:2 (Apr.): 324–335.

———. 2014. *Place and Politics in Latin American Digital Culture: Location and Latin American Net Art*. New York: Routledge.

Turok, Neil. 2012. *The Universe Within: From Quantum to Cosmos*. Toronto: House of Anansi Press.

———. 2012. "The Universe Within." *CBC Radio. Massey Lecture Series: Ideas*. November. Accesssed November 12, 2012. www.cbc.ca/ideas/episodes.

"urb." 2014. *Dictionary.com Unabridged*. Random House, Inc. Accessed August 1, 2014. Dictionary.com. http://dictionary.reference.com/browse/urb

Urriola, Malú and Nadia Prado. 2003. "Neoliberalismo, fabulaciones y complot." *Revista de Crítica Cultural* 26 (June): 1-2.

——— 2004. *Poesía es +*. Santiago: Editorial Surada.

Valdés, Mario J. 1994. "The Invention of Reality: Hispanic Postmodernism." *Revista Canadiense de Estudios Hispánicos* 18, No. 3 (Spring): 455–468.

———. 1992. *World-making: The Literary Truth-Claim and the Interpretation of Texts*. Toronto: University of Toronto Press.

Valdez, Pedro Antonio. 1999. *La bachata del ángel caído*. San Juan/Santo Domingo: Isla Negra Editores.

Valenzuela, Luis P. 2004. " Copyright de Nadia Prado: Simulacro y palabra de un cuerpo nefasto." August 31. Accessed June 15, 2012. www.sobrelibros.cl

Valerio Holguín, Fernando. 2000. "Bolero, historia e identidad en Ritos de cabaret de Marcio Veloz Maggiolo." *Crítica Hispánica* 22 (1-2): 194–203.

———. 2002a. "El bolero en la narrativa latinoamericana." *Xinesquema* 2: 131–140.

———. 2008. "El orden de la música popular en la narrative dominicana." *Céfiro* 8:1 (Spring): 101–118.

———. 1999. "Jacques Lacan, Lucho Gatica y Pedro Vergés: el Imaginario bolerístico en *Sólo cenizas hallarás (Bolero)*." *La Torre: Revista de la Universidad de Puerto Rico* 4 (11): 109–120.

———. 2002b. "La historia como 'causa ausente' en *Sólo cenizas hallarás (Bolero)* de Pedro Vergés." *Revista Hispánica Moderna* 53 (1): 206–13.

Varcárcel, Eva. 1997. "La borra del café: La escritura y la memoria." In *Mario Benedetti: Inventario Cómplice* by Carmen Alemany, Remedios Mataix and José Carlos Rovira. Alicante. *Biblioteca Virtual Miguel de Cervantes*. www.cervantesvirtual.com/obra-visor/mario-benedetti-inventario-complice--0/html/ff1470c0-82b1-11df-acc7- 002185ce6064_121.html#I_155_

Veloz Maggiolo, Marcio. 1991. *Ritos de Cabaret (Novela rítmica)*. Santo Domingo: Editora Taller.

———. 2003. *El hombre del acordeón*. Madrid: Ediciones Siruela.

Vergés, Pedro. 1981. *Sólo cenizas hallarás (Bolero)*. 2nd Edition. Barcelona: Ediciones Destino.

Vicuña, Cecilia. 2013. In "The Poetics of Performance." A Conversation of Rosa Alcalá and Cecilia Vicuña. Recorded in New York on February 8th after the presentation of *Spit Temple*. Accessed October 24, 2013. http://vimeo.com/77621895

———. 2012. *The Selected Performances of Cecilia Vicuña*. Edited and translated by Rosa Alcalá New York: Ugly Duckling Presse.

———. 1999. *Cloud-Net.* Translated by Rosa Alcalá. Essays by Surpik Angelini, Laura Hoptman and David Levi Strauss. New York, N.Y.: Art in General.

———. 2012. "Hilo de agua, hilo de vida." [Son of Water, Son of Life] (Performance) XXII Congress of the Asociación Internacional de Literatura y Cultura Femenina Hispánica (AILFCH). "De la tierra al ciberespacio / Between the Earth and Cyberspace." Grand Valley State University. Grand Rapids, Michigan. November 9.

———. 2006. "A Menstrual Quipu: The Blood of the Glaciers Journal. [El Quipu Menstrual]." November 17. Part of the installation "The Other Side, Chilean Women Artists in the Centro Cultural Palacio de la Moneda. Santiago, Chile. November 9 to December 31, 2006." Centro Cultural Palacio de la Moneda, West Gallery, Plaza de la Ciudadanía, 26 Santiago Centro. www.ccplm.cl Web. August 8, 2014. www.ceciliavicuna.org/en_exhibition.htm

———. 2012. *Spit Temple*. Edited and translated by Rosa Alcalá. New York: Ugly Duckling Presse. www.uglyducklingpresse.org/wpcontent/uploads/2014/01/Spit_Temple_Free.pdf

Viglietti, Daniel and Mario Benedetti. 2007. *Desalambrando*. Buenos Aires: Seix Barral.

Walker, Michele Boulous. 1998. *Philosophy and the maternal body: Reading silence*. New York: Routledge.

Yépez, Heriberto. 2013. *The Empire of Neomemory*. Translated from Spanish by Jen Hofer, Christian Nager, and Brian Whitener. Oakland/Philadelphia: Chain Links.

———. 2007. *El imperio de la neomemoria*, Oaxaca: Almadía.

Yúdice, George. 2003. *The Expediency of Culture: Uses of Culture in the Global Era*. Durham, NC: Duke University Press.

Zoé, Valdés. 2006. *Bailar con la vida*. Barcelona: Planeta.

www.ingramcontent.com/pod-product-compliance
Lightning Source LLC
Chambersburg PA
CBHW062027290426
44108CB00025B/2807

www.ingramcontent.com/pod-product-compliance
Lightning Source LLC
Chambersburg PA
CBHW070723020526
44116CB00031B/1465